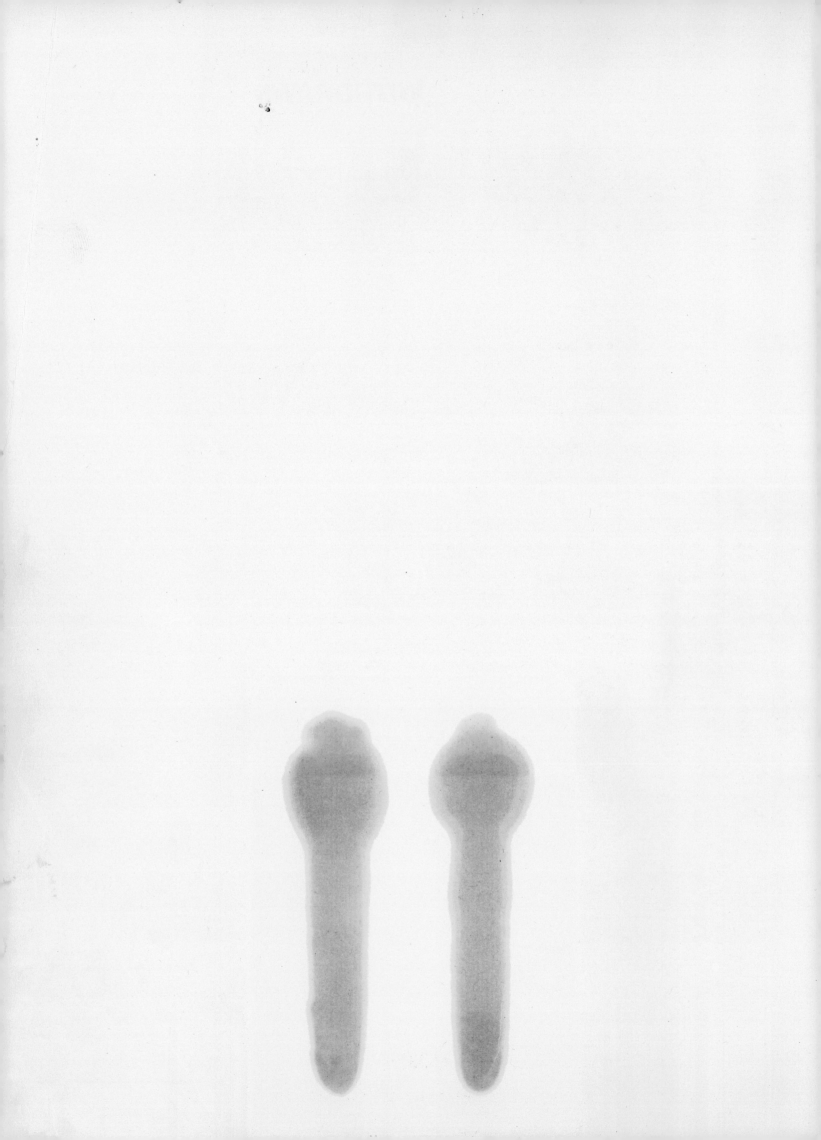

THE ANTIQUES BOOK OF

AMERICAN INTERIORS

COLONIAL & FEDERAL STYLES

Overleaf: Dining room, Kenmore, Fredericksburg, Virginia, 1752-56.

THE ANTIQUES BOOK OF
AMERICAN INTERIORS
COLONIAL & FEDERAL STYLES

COMPILED BY ELISABETH DONAGHY GARRETT

Crown Publishers, Inc., New York

Contents

Introduction

To successive generations of eighteenth- and nineteenth-century Americans, the home—their own as well as that of their friends—defined their social and economic standing. In most Colonial and Federal villages all entertainment sanctioned by fashionable society took place in the home. Reading books, visiting friends, playing cards, drinking tea and spirits, and dining enlivened the parlors and dining rooms. Sarah Anna Emery recalled her pleasurable girlhood in post-Revolutionary Newburyport, Massachusetts:

> My cousin and myself were now fairly launched on the sea of fashionable life . . . Luxurious indolence, rich dinners, with long sittings over the wine and dessert, card parties of an evening with a hot meat supper at nine or ten o'clock, was the usual routine in many of our first families.

Sarah Emery further elaborated on the routine of the day, underscoring the pivotal role of the parlor in creating a hospitable home:

> The morning was usually devoted to making calls and the reception of visitors, when the on-dits of the day, and the last novel, were discussed over a bit of cake and a glass of wine. The afternoons passed in practising a new tune, reading a new book, or working at some dainty needlework . . . The evenings, when not spent abroad, or in formal parties at home, were enlivened by social calls from gentlemen friends, who talked politics with my uncle . . . discussed books, or sang and flirted with Mira and myself.

Nancy Shippen's Philadelphia journal book reveals a very similar round of days and evenings spent in the most important of the Colonial and Federal rooms—the parlor. Even of the country, where farming and household demands precluded such a succession of social hours, and where luxury was often strictly rationed, William Cobbett could observe that "The first business of a farmer is here, and ought to be everywhere, to live well: to live in ease and plenty; to 'keep hospitality,' as the old English saying was." Mary Palmer Tyler of Guilford, Vermont, recalled: "The monotony of our lives was varied and enlivened by the genuine spirit of hospitality inherent, I believe, in all new countries where caste is unknown, and neighbors are neighbors indeed. The winter season witnessed almost weekly a feast at some of the houses within our circle."

The interior decoration of the upper-class home from the mid-eighteenth century to the first several decades of the nineteenth, the period during which most of the houses included in this volume were built, reflected the conservative and measured taste of the well-bred provincial of British background. The American paterfamilias and his wife required that all the furnishings be skillfully made of handsome materials, that they be "neat" (to use the language of the time). "There were no cheap shops in those days, no five cent counters," recalled Caroline King of Salem, Massachusetts, in obvious reference to the mid-century emporium which brought mass-produced goods to every city and village in the country. In the period of her youth, in the early years of the century, "You paid the worth of what you bought," she reminisced, "and it was a matter of honor to the salesman that his goods should be what they professed to be. Strict honesty was the law of those shops."

The Georgian Colonial style, widely introduced in North America in the early years of the eighteenth century, was that which set the framework for interior decoration until at least the 1790s. The Georgian style was characterized by a much less harsh aesthetic than that of the early Colonial which reflected the rigors of settlement and the flat, two-dimensional lines of the post-Reformation world. The Georgian was curvilinear in profile, employing the bolection molding, the gently-raised panel, the broken pediment. In furniture forms, the movement was from the softly-shaped curves of the Queen Anne side chair to the more elaborately carved and shaped block-front or bombé Chippendale chest. The Federal style of the period from 1790 through the succeeding thirty years (it continued in vogue beyond the Eastern seaboard until well into the 1840s), was a continuation of the symmetrical mode established earlier but with an increased emphasis on neoclassical formality. The American Federal style was more subdued and rectilinear in composition. Ornament was reduced and concentrated in fewer places in the parlor and dining room. Furniture assumed straight lines and solid forms under the influence of Thomas Sheraton and Robert Adam in the years 1790-1810, and then in design moved in the direction of the scrolled line. Duncan Phyfe, who employed as many as 100 workmen in his New York shop during the early 1800s, popularized such forms as the outcurved lyre-splat back chair and the window seat and sofa with outscrolled arms.

Craftsmen such as Phyfe, the Salem carver and builder Samuel McIntire, and earlier furniture makers such as Benjamin Randolph and Thomas Affleck of Philadelphia were patronized by the well-to-do. "The Lindens" (pp. 96-107), built in 1754 for Robert "King" Hooper in Danvers, Massachusetts, is typical of the Georgian Colonial homes furnished by true artisans whose work was "neat," not at all "cheap," and certainly honest. The first Harrison Gray Otis House (pp. 108-119), built in 1795 in Boston, can well stand as a representative Federal-style structure. As restored by the Society for the Preservation of New England Antiquities, it reflects in its woodwork, papers, mantelpieces, window hangings, and furniture the neoclassical refinement which is the hallmark of the period.

During the eighteenth and early-nineteenth centuries, before home furnishings were mass produced, interior decoration was quite proscribed. The variation to be found in one home in the Georgian or Federal periods from another home in the same style was only in quality or quantity. The wide selection of goods available to the home decorator today was unknown. Alexander Mackay found that in Philadelphia "private residences in the fashionable quarters are large and exceedingly comodious; but such is the sameness in their internal arrangements, that when you have seen one, you have virtually seen all."

The decoration of the handcrafted interior changed only slowly and almost imperceptibly between 1750 and 1820. Rich Colonial colors faded to Republican pastels; furniture was lightened in form and color; and carpets covered the floors of fashionable parlors and dining rooms by the opening years of the nineteenth century. The arrangement of furniture and the pieces of furniture one would expect to find in each room, nevertheless, changed little in time. Furniture of an earlier period was mixed with that of a later time.

Order in the tasteful late-Colonial and Federal interior was imposed by an almost immutable law: furniture was to be arranged against the wall in the accepted tradition of seventeenth-century France and thence England. In the parlor, the core of the house, primly arranged chairs —frequently in sets of twelve—tables, and perhaps a sofa outlined the walls. Harmony in the room was further achieved by the accord of fabric colors and textures. Chairs and sofas were to conform in color with the window treatment in a sophisticated interior. A table might stand in the pier formed by two windows, frequently with a looking glass suspended above. Worktables, card tables, and tea tables were brought out into the room for use and returned to their border positions afterward. Although memoirs and diaries make frequent note of drawing a table out into the room, there is never a reference to returning it, an omission that suggests the important role of servants in prosperous surroundings.

Servants helped to keep a table top neatly covered with a coth or polished until it reflected light like a mirror.

Table surfaces were kept free of ornament until around 1820, when books, a lamp, or a small and tightly-arranged bouquet might rest on the polished top. Household help was also needed in a large house where fires required laying and maintaining for cooking and heating, where light was obtained from guttering candles and only later from lamps that consumed whale oil in an inefficient burner.

The eighteenth- and early-nineteenth-century interior was a study in chiaroscuro. As evening darkened the rooms, light was primarily seen as the glint of polished wood surfaces, the glitter of brass tacks defining the outlines of a sofa or swagged across the seats of a row of chairs, the glimmer of gilded picture frames and looking glasses suspended so as to reflect a maximum of light, the gloss of glazed cottons, watered silks, and multi-faceted brocades.

The historic interiors of the Colonial and Federal periods chronicled in *The Magazine Antiques* over a span of more than fifty years are by no means typical. They are among the best of two periods that seen together can only be called admirable in craftsmanship and proportion. And they are the exemplars of taste which served then and serve now as testimony of the grace and harmony which can be achieved by the artistry of men. As homes —places where real people performed daily domestic duties, entertained, and played out their lives—these buildings have a special feeling and fascination. "Home is the place that comes first to mind when America remembers," wrote Samuel Rapport and Patricia Schartle in the introduction to their book *America Remembers.* Preeminent among America's historic homes, of course, is the White House. An institution of mythical proportions, it has remained, nevertheless, the home of a family. Clement E. Conger's survey, "Decorative Arts at the White House" (pp. 132-154), explains how and in what manner this most symbolic house has been carefully furnished in recent years.

Each home or group of interiors illustrated in this volume—including such masterpieces as "Middleton" (pp. 61-77), near Charleston, South Carolina; the William Paca House (pp. 8-10), in Annapolis, Maryland; or the exemplary period rooms of the Henry Francis du Pont Winterthur Museum (pp. 22-60), near Wilmington, Delaware—provides an instructive lesson in period interior decoration. Presented almost completely in full color, the extraordinary richness of the best woods, fabrics, papers, floor coverings, and paints of the time and how they were combined to form a harmonious whole can be completely conveyed and enjoyed.

The restoration of
the interior of the William Paca House

BY RUSSELL J. WRIGHT

TWO MAJOR DECISIONS had to be made before the interior of the William Paca House was restored: a use had to be found for the house commensurate with its importance, and a plan had to be made for its maintenance, since Historic Annapolis, Incorporated has no endowment. The decision to use the house as a house museum as well as a reception center for distinguished visitors and for conferences satisfied both objectives. It also revived Annapolis' historic role as a port of entry for foreigners and as a meeting place for officials, first of the colony, then of the state of Maryland. The museum is on the main floor; guest bedrooms are on the second floor and in the wings; a small conference room is in the above-ground basement; and modern conveniences are tucked away in the hyphens and in other out-of-the-way areas.

The decision was made to restore the house as accurately as possible to its appearance between about 1765 and 1780, the years of Paca's residence. This led to intensive studies undertaken for Historic Annapolis, first by the archaeologist Stanley South and later by consultants and the staff of Historic Annapolis. The board of directors decided that archaeological and architectural research would take precedence over demolition and restoration so far as scheduling and funding were concerned. While this arrangement has

required dedication and patience by all who have participated in the project, the accuracy and authenticity of the restoration and the thrill of discovering even the most minor original architectural details far outweigh the inconveniences and delays.

Research began before Carvel Hall, the 1907 hotel which encompassed the house, was torn down, and was intensified after the demolition of the hotel's powerhouse. The ensuing removal of the electrical, plumbing, and heating systems of the Paca House made archaeological study much easier. This research revealed what a surprisingly large number of original architectural features were intact, considering the commercial uses to which the building had been put.

Research was carried on for five years before any restoration was attempted. The studies comprised on-site exploration of the interior architecture of the house; comparison of its features with those found in contemporary design books, as well as with similar features in contemporary Annapolis houses; stripping sometimes as many as twenty layers of paint; Stanley South's archaeological report of 1967; and a careful study of old photographs of the house.

The removal of plaster in certain areas contributed to the discovery that all the fireplace openings on the main floor had been altered with the exception of that in a small room under the stairs. The fireplace in the parlor (color plate) had been reduced on at least two occasions, and when it was opened to its original size it was found that the elaborately carved mantel would nearly fit inside the fireplace opening, proving that it was not the first mantel used in this room. Research revealed that the design of the mantel was taken directly from Plate LXI of Batty Langley's *The City and Country Builder's and Workman's Treasury of Designs* (London, 1741 edition). Further research proved that William Buckland, who was working on a number of projects in Annapolis while the Paca House was being built, owned a copy of the 1741 edition of Langley's *Builder's Treasury*, among other eighteenth-century builders' handbooks. This suggests that the mantel was made locally if not by Buckland himself. It is probable that the mantel was installed during the 1770's when, it appears from other evidence, the elaborate cornice and overmantel were added. However, because of the importance of the surviving eighteenth-century mantel, its relationship to other architectural details in the room, and the lack of evidence as to the appearance of the original, the fireplace opening was reduced, and the mantel reinstalled.

The early twentieth-century mantels in the rooms now known as the "dining room" and the "hall" were removed and the fireplace openings restored to their original size. New mantels were designed for these two rooms, based on a comparative analysis of mantels in other Annapolis

Fig. 1. Chinese-trellis-pattern balustrade leading from the second floor to the attic of the William Paca House. *Photographs are by M. E. Warren.*

Parlor of the Paca House.

Fig. 2. X-ray photograph of the newel post and two balusters of the main staircase leading from the main to the second floor. The wrought nails attaching the newel post to the handrail and the wrought, cut, and modern wire nails attaching the turned balusters to the handrail indicate that this stair was originally constructed in the eighteenth century, but has been repaired or reassembled in more recent years.

houses of the period, the window and door frames in the rooms, designs in Langley's *Builder's Treasury*, and the carved mantel in the parlor. The final fireplace on this floor, in the small room under the stairs, was investigated for signs of a mantel or shelf; but while the original nailing blocks remained in place, no nail holes were found in them, and they had been plastered over with the rest of the wall. Thus, this fireplace has been left as found, without a mantel.

The removal of the frame and plaster on the fireplace in the bedroom above the parlor revealed that the original segmental-arch opening had been modified. The heavily molded fireplace surround found in the room is not original, since it is not tall enough to accommodate the original opening. Moreover, a study of the paint in the room revealed that the first layer of paint on the mantel did not match the original color of the wood trim. However, an analysis of saw cuts and nails indicated that the fireplace surround was probably built before 1800. Thus, because of its compatible design and a reluctance to remove an early alteration, it has been retained.

A study of the paint and nails showed that the mantel and fireplace opening in the bedroom over the dining room were original. The mantel includes a curious one-inch overhang along one edge that accepts the chair rail. The mantel and fireplace opening in the bedroom over the hall had been altered, but research showed that they had originally matched those in the bedroom over the dining room, and they were restored in that way.

Fig. 3. This restored arch is based on a design in Batty Langley, *The City and Country Builder's and Workman's Treasury of Designs* (London, 1750), Pl. XXI. The fluted and reeded pilasters are original.

The cast-plaster cornice in the parlor was added in two horizontal bands, each using plaster of a different composition. Nailing blocks extending below the lower band indicate that a deeper wooden cornice was intended instead of the plaster one. It is not known whether the wooden cornice was ever installed, although it can be said that there are no nail holes in the nailing blocks. An analysis of the paint on the cornice failed to determine when either band was executed, but it was found that the top band and the cast-plaster overmantel are of the same date. It seems probable that the plastering was done eight to ten years after construction began on the house, for there is a record of William Buckland borrowing five hundred pounds of stucco from Paca sometime between 1771 and 1774.* Examination of the parlor overmantel also revealed the outline of a surrounding design of garlands, cartouches, and pineapples which was probably cast in composition and applied. These ornamental elements have been duplicated.

The windows in the parlor and in the hall were originally designed to incorporate window seats similar to those found in the main-floor rooms at the rear of the house and throughout the second floor, but at some early point the windows were extended to the floor. The design of the fixed, full-length reveals almost exactly duplicates that of the interior shutters used in the Chase-Lloyd house. Unfortunately, the upper sections of the Paca House reveals were stolen in the 1960's, but they have been restored based on the remaining soffits and on photographic evidence. Photographs were also the key to the restoration of the original staircase from the parlor to the west hyphen with its Chinese-trellis-pattern balustrade.

An investigation of the main staircase involved all the research techniques as well as X ray. X rays of the nails and the details of the joinery indicated that the balustrade from the second floor to the attic appears to be original

*James Bordley Jr., "New Light on William Buckland," *Maryland Historical Magazine*, vol. 46 (1951), pp. 153-154.

to the house, but that the balustrade on the second-floor landing is made with cut rather than wrought nails, and therefore is of a slightly later date (Fig. 1). Historical research showed that it was customary in Maryland houses for this Chinese-trellis-pattern balustrade to extend to the main floor rather than terminate, as it does at the Paca House, at the second floor. The stairway from the second to the main floor consists of a molded handrail supported by turned mahogany balusters of pre-1800 construction, three to a stair. This design too is often found in early Maryland houses, but in the Paca House the balusters and handrail have been reset several times (Fig. 2). Both balusters and handrail are either original to the house or from another house of the same period. Since it has proved impossible to determine whether the Chinese-trellis-pattern balustrade originally extended from the second to the main floor, the turned-baluster balustrade has been retained.

Other restorations to the house include reinstalling a partition between the dining room and the hall; constructing cornices in the dining room and hall that duplicate the cornice in the front hall; and reconstructing the arch that spans the front hall (Fig. 3) which had been altered early in the twentieth century. The kitchen wing on the east of the house retains its original brick fireplaces, paneled stairway, and an interesting eighteenth-century garbage-disposal system. Although sufficient archaeological evidence was uncovered to restore completely William Paca's wine cellar, necessity dictated that this space be used to house heating, lighting, and air-conditioning equipment. The pain of this decision was lessened by the fact that eighteenth-century wine cellars still exist intact in several other Annapolis mansions.

The restoration of the Paca House was an unusually large research project that was carefully documented by photographs, X rays, paint analyses, field notes, drawings of elevations, and archaeological stratigraphy. It is hoped that Historic Annapolis will, in time, be able to publish this research as a guide to others faced with the necessity of salvaging an irreplaceable national historic landmark.

The Jonathan Sayward House, York, Maine

BY RICHARD C. NYLANDER, *Curator of collections*
Society for the Preservation of New England Antiquities

THE EXTERIOR of the Jonathan Sayward House in York, Maine, is typical of many houses built in that coastal town in the first half of the eighteenth century (Pl. I, Figs. 1, 2). The style is derived from local building traditions, not from the more formal designs in the English architectural pattern books that were used elsewhere in the Colonies at the time. Despite its unassuming exterior, the house is of great importance to students of both the decorative arts and social history, for in it is a collection of superbly documented furnishings, most of which date from the mid-eighteenth century and are original to the house.

The building was described as "a New Dwelling House" when Joseph Sayward (1684–1741), a millwright, purchased it from Noah Peck in 1720.[1] Sayward was active in civic affairs and was an elder of the Congregational church, but he was imprudent in his financial affairs, and in 1732 the town of York voted to help him out of the debt in which he had "been for some years much involved."[2] Perhaps to provide further financial aid, Jonathan Sayward purchased the house from his father in 1735 for £200. After the elder Sayward's death in 1741, Jonathan Sayward lived in the house with his first wife, Sarah, and his mother, who died in 1759.

According to the diary Sayward began in 1760 and kept almost until his death,[3] in November 1761 he paid £45 to Samuel Sewell, a local joiner, "towards

Fig. 1. Southwest façade of the Jonathan Sayward House, built c. 1720, York, Maine. *Photographs are by J. David Bohl.*

Pl. I. View of the Sayward House by Lucretia Peabody Hale (1820–1900), late nineteenth century. Watercolor on paper, 8⅞ by 11¼ inches. In the eighteenth century Jonathan Sayward's wharf was in front of the house, and his sawmill was on a tidal pond directly behind the house.

Pl. II. Jonathan Sayward (1713–1797), artist unknown, c. 1775. Oil on canvas, 57 by 46 inches. According to family tradition, this portrait and an unfinished companion portrait of Sayward's first wife, Sarah Mitchell (see Pl. III), were painted by an English artist. The painter is said to have fled when it was rumored that the Sayward house would be mobbed, but a more logical reason for the unfinished state of Mrs. Sayward's portrait is her death in 1775.

his work on my House." This work probably included installing the paneling which survives in the parlor (Fig. 4) and in the room above it (Pl. X). In 1767 Sayward added a small bedroom on the first floor (Pl. VII), but otherwise there have been no major alterations to the house in the past two hundred-odd years.

Jonathan Sayward referred to himself in deeds and other documents as a "trader," a "coaster," and a "marriner." In 1744 Governor William Shirley of Massachusetts commissioned him to command the sloop *Sea Flower* in the expedition against Cape Breton Island, Nova Scotia, which resulted in the capture of the French fortress at Louisburg in 1745. By about 1760 Sayward had built up a substantial shipping business, and in succeeding years he was involved in the lumber trade with the West Indies and the fur trade with Canada. His business contacts had been strengthened by the marriage in 1758 of his only child, Sarah, to the aspiring merchant Nathaniel Barrell—a brother of the better-known Boston merchant Joseph Barrell.[4] Nathaniel Barrell went alone to England in 1760 to establish trade contacts, and his wife and daughter Sally, the first of eleven children, moved in with his wife's parents in York. After Barrell's return in 1763, he and his family lived on a farm Sayward owned at Beech Ridge, a few miles up the York River from his own house.

Fig. 2. East façade of the Sayward House in a photograph taken before 1883. Elizabeth (1799–1883) and Mary Barrell (1803–1889), the daughters of Jonathan Sayward Barrell and Mary Plummer Barrell (Fig. 6), stand in the doorway.

Sayward was adamant in his loyalty to England before and during the Revolution.[5] He was York's representative to the General Court in 1766 and 1768. In the latter year he was included as one of the seventeen Rescinders depicted in Paul Revere's famous broadside.[6] Sayward's vote in favor of the crown lost him the esteem of his constituency, however, and in 1775 all his political offices were taken from him. He described that year in his diary as one "of Extraordinary trials": his business suffered greatly; his wife died; and he was confined to York. However, according to the diary, he lived in such fear of being driven out of town that he carried £200 in his pocket at all times.

In 1778 Sayward's granddaughter Sally Sayward Barrell (1759–1855) married his apprentice Richard Keating,[7] and they moved in with him. The following year Sayward himself married Elizabeth Plummer of Gloucester, Massachusetts. In the 1780's and 1790's he often visited friends in Boston and entertained others at his house in York. He noted in his diary in 1788 that his estate was diminishing, but he continued to take on apprentices to work in his warehouses. One of these was his eldest grandson and namesake, Jonathan Sayward Barrell, who attended Dummer Academy in Newbury, Massachusetts, and then returned to York in 1786 to work for his grandfather. In 1795 Sayward Barrell, as he was called, married Elizabeth Sayward's niece Mary Plummer and set out to establish himself as a prosperous merchant.

When Jonathan Sayward died, on May 8, 1797, at the age of eighty-four, he bequeathed to Sayward Barrell his house and its contents. Specifically mentioned in the will were the tall-case clock shown in Plate V, a map of North America, and "the Family & other Pictures."[8] He provided his wife with the use of the northwest part of the house during her widowhood and gave her outright enough furniture for her comfort. The only piece of furniture bequeathed to anyone living outside the house was a bed he left to his daughter, Sarah, "to use and dispose of as she pleases."[9]

Sayward Barrell's ill luck as a merchant kept the house from being much altered during the nineteenth century. Fragments of wallpaper of the Federal period and a few pieces of Federal furniture indicate that the house was to some extent redecorated in the early years of the nineteenth century. However, Jefferson's embargo of 1807 and the War of 1812 destroyed Barrell's financial stability, and he came to operate a local store.

The eight Barrell children were well educated, but money was in short supply and it was a constant struggle to keep the house in the family. In 1822 Barrell was forced to mortgage the house to Theodore Lyman, a friend who was living in Waltham, Massachusetts. It continued to be mortgaged to members of the family or friends until the mid-nineteenth century. In 1822 Barrell sold to his daughter Elizabeth most of the furnishings in the house in order to pay the legacies from an estate of which he was executor.

The primary documentation for the furnishings in the house today are the list of objects in that sale and the objects listed in Jonathan Sayward's will.

Elizabeth Barrell and her sister Mary took on the responsibilities of the household early in life. Their mother had died in 1814 and their stepmother, Anna Plummer (their mother's sister), in 1826. They remained at home after their brothers left, and cared for their father until his death in 1857. Through the generosity of their brother Joseph, they received title to the house in 1841. With the money received from the sale of Jonathan Sayward's sawmill in 1859, they made repairs to the house and some minor alterations to the ell. They took great pride showing the house of their "venerable ancestor" to visitors, and it is apparent that their reverence for it prevented them from even rearranging objects within the house, especially in the parlor (compare Pl. III and Fig. 3).

At Mary Barrell's death in 1889, the house was left to her only nephew, George Octavius Barrell (1848–1900). The inventory of her estate indicates that a sofa, a rocking chair, and stoves were among the few furnishings that had been added since the list made in 1822.

Pl. III.   On the walls of the parlor hang portraits of Jonathan Sayward (Pl. II), his first wife, Sarah (d. 1775), both painted by the same unknown artist c. 1775, and a portrait of their only child, Sarah (Mrs. Nathaniel Barrell; 1738–1805), painted by Joseph Blackburn (w. 1752–1774) in 1761. (See also ANTIQUES for November 1978, p. 944.) The Sayward coat of arms between the portraits of the ladies was painted by John Gore (1718–1796), 1765–1770. The mahogany drop-leaf table was made in the Portsmouth, New Hampshire, region, c. 1760. The three side chairs were also made in the Portsmouth region, 1760–1770, and retain their original harrateen upholstery. They are part of the set of "six mahogany chairs, seated with Green" that Jonathan Sayward bequeathed to his second wife, Elizabeth Plummer, in 1797. Under the English mahogany looking glass, c. 1780, is a mahogany tea table made in Massachusetts c. 1760. On it stands an English tea chest that Jonathan Sayward bought from the Boston merchant John Scollay in 1759. The brass hot-water urn on the mahogany pedestal table in the corner was given to Jonathan Sayward by Sir William Pepperrell, the commander of the 1744–1745 expedition against Cape Breton Island, in appreciation of Sayward's participation in the capture of Louisburg. The wallpaper, installed in 1953, is a reproduction of a French paper of c. 1809.

Fig. 3. Parlor in a photograph taken c. 1875. With the exception of the mirror above the tea table, the carpet, and the wallpaper, all the objects shown in this view remain in the house, most of them in this room (see Pl. III). According to a description of the house published in 1869, the room then "contained numerous curiosities. . . . Three full-length oil paintings were hung at the end of the room. . . . They were the family of Saywards, ancestors of the present residents. The colors of those old paintings, although executed so long ago, were as fresh as if put on but yesterday. The family coat-of-arms hung on the mantle; and below it were old engravings of the commanders of the English Army and Navy in 1760. . . . A long damask curtain was drawn away from a recess at one corner of the room, displaying an elegant set of ancient India China and other curiosities of the last century. Among them was a brass tea urn taken at the capture of Louisburg. This room . . . was filled with ancient furniture. Club-footed chairs, quaintly formed tables and sofa carried one back to the days of yore when York was one of the busiest seaport towns on the coast" (*Historical Magazine and Notes and Queries Concerning the Antiquities, History, and Biography of America* [August 1869], vol. 6, p. 101).

Pl. IV. This corner cupboard in the parlor, called a "bofat" in an inventory of 1884, is referred to in a description of the room in 1869 (see Fig. 3), when the enameled cloak pins held back a "long damask curtain" (see Pl. XII). In 1841 Jonathan Sayward's granddaughter Sally identified the round Chinese porcelain plates decorated with red and blue as those that her grandfather brought back as booty from the Louisburg expedition of 1744–1745. The Chinese octagonal porcelain plates and charger were brought from England by Nathaniel Barrell in 1763. Most of the glassware is English of the mid- and late eighteenth century.

Fig. 4. The paneling on the fireplace wall of the parlor was probably installed in 1761 and was originally painted olive green. The prints were published by Jonathan Bowles and Son of London in the mid-eighteenth century. Many New England inventories of the eighteenth century suggest that prints were often clustered over a fireplace.

Fig. 5. The massive mahogany sideboard in the sitting room (see also Pl. V) is one of the few pieces of Federal furniture added to the house by Jonathan Sayward Barrell. Above it hangs a portrait of his father, Nathaniel Barrell (1732–1831), painted by John Coles Jr. (1776 or 1780–1854) in 1816. On either side of the portrait are engravings from the Shakespeare series published in London by John (1719–1804) and Josiah (c. 1750–1817) Boydell in the late eighteenth century. The earlier engravings of European scenes above the mantel are four of "8 old pictures in frames (small)" listed in the 1784 inventory of Richard Keating. The name of Keating's wife, Sally Sayward Keating, and the initials of her grandfather, Jonathan Sayward, are incised in the frames.

In 1900 the house and contents were purchased by Elizabeth Cheever Wheeler, a direct descendant of Jonathan Sayward who had visited the house frequently when it was occupied by the Barrell sisters. Without detracting from the architectural integrity of the exterior, she added a porch and dormers on the ell to accommodate bathrooms. The character of the interior was retained as well, although the woodwork was painted white, the walls were repapered, and straw matting was laid on the floors. Mrs. Wheeler and her family summered in the house until 1977, when her heirs presented it to the Society for the Preservation of New England Antiquities, respecting her desire that house and contents be preserved "as a unified whole." The house was formally opened to the public on July 8, 1978, and it may be visited in the summer.

Pl. V. The sitting room is the largest room in the house, and was probably used frequently for entertaining. However, as late as the 1790's Jonathan Sayward recorded in his diary that he moved his bed into this room in the winter. The mahogany tall-case clock, possibly made in Portsmouth, New Hampshire, is screwed to a rough plank, which in turn is nailed to the corner post with hand-wrought nails. The central finial, removed so that the clock would fit, is still preserved in the room. During the restless nights before the Revolution Sayward noted in his diary that he heard the clock strike every hour. The black-walnut side chairs were made in the Portsmouth region c. 1760. The English walnut looking glass of about the same date retains its original glass and is secured to the wall by the original hardware. The cornice has been cut to accommodate the top of the frame. The mahogany drop-leaf table of c. 1770 was made in the Portsmouth region.

Pl. VI. An early eighteenth-century maple slant-front desk possibly made in York stands in the stair hall. The portrait, of 1740–1750, is oil on paper and may be by Joseph Badger (1708–1765). The subject was identified by Elizabeth and Mary Barrell as Penelope Winslow and a companion portrait on the opposite wall as being of her brother John. The Winslows are thought to have been loyalists who fled to Halifax. The mahogany chair of 1760–1770 was made in the Portsmouth region and is one of a set of six. Some of the chairs in the set are still upholstered in the same green harrateen as the more elaborate set of chairs in the parlor (see Pl. III).

Pl. VII. The early nineteenth-century mahogany bed in the small first-floor bedroom is hung with eighteenth-century blue-check linen bound with linen tape. The hangings may have been made from the "piece of check" that Jonathan Sayward recorded in his diary as having been bought in Kittery, Maine, in 1771. Over the mantel hangs the Barrell family coat of arms painted on velvet, 1810–1820. The walnut slant-front desk of c. 1780 was made in New England. On it is a box stamped on the top *GR*, indicating that it may have been a souvenir of George III's coronation. That event was witnessed by Nathaniel Barrell, who brought the box from England in 1763.

Pl. VIII. The room above the sitting room is the only major one in the house that retains its original woodwork. The black-walnut-veneered high chest of drawers with sumac inlay was made in the York region, 1735–1745. The embroidered covers on the maple stools beneath it were worked by Jonathan Sayward's granddaughter Sally Sayward Barrell. The black-walnut easy chair was originally upholstered by Samuel Grant (1705–1784) of Boston and was shipped to Jonathan Sayward by the Boston merchant John Scollay in 1759. On the mantel is a pair of milk-glass lamps, c. 1830, marked by the New England Glass Company of East Cambridge, Massachusetts.

[1] York Deeds, Book X, fol. 29, in the York County Courthouse, Alfred, Maine. I am indebted to Alice Gray Reed, whose research significantly added to what was known about Jonathan Sayward, his house, and its place in York's history.

[2] Quoted in Charles A. Sayward, *The Sayward Family* (Ipswich, Massachusetts, 1890), p. 50.

[3] The diary was given to the American Antiquarian Society, Worcester, Massachusetts, by Leonard Wheeler.

[4] While Joseph Barrell is the best-known member of this family of eighteenth-century merchants, it is apparent that he was only part of a trade network which included his father and nine brothers, each of whom established himself in a major seaport in the Colonies and one of whom served as the family's agent in London.

[5] For more detailed accounts of Sayward's political career, see Charles Edward Banks, *History of York Maine* (Boston, 1931), pp. 389-401; and John Cary, "'The Juditious Are Intirely Neglected': The Fate of a Tory," to be published in a forthcoming issue of *The New England Historic and Genealogical Register*.

[6] The broadside, entitled *A Warm Place—Hell*, was published in 1768 and is reproduced and discussed in Clarence S. Brigham, *Paul Revere's Engravings* (Worcester, Massachusetts, 1954), pp. 35-38.

[7] Keating died in 1783, leaving his widow with a son and two daughters. In 1804 his widow married General Abiel Wood (d. 1811). Known as Madam Wood, she was Maine's first woman novelist.

[8] York County Register of Probate, vol. 17, p. 345, no. 16674, York County Courthouse.

[9] *Ibid.*

Fig. 6. Double silhouette of Jonathan Sayward Barrell (1772–1857) and his first wife, Mary Plummer Barrell (1771–1814), by William King (w. 1804–1809). See also Pl. X.

Pl. IX. The paneled fireplace wall of the room above the kitchen originally continued across the width of the room, making a small room of the alcove at the right. Another partition, removed in 1900, divided the room in half. The painted pine and ash table of 1750–1775 is one of several in the house. The windsor chair is from one of two sets in the house.

Pl. X. The paneling in this room is similar to that on the fireplace wall of the parlor directly below (see Fig. 4). The mahogany chest of drawers, 1760–1770, was probably made in York, and may be the "Bearough" mentioned in Jonathan Sayward's will of 1797. Over it hangs a mahogany looking glass of c. 1790 made in England. The double silhouette (Fig. 6) of Jonathan Sayward Barrell and his first wife, Mary Plummer, is surrounded by silhouettes of five of their eight children.

Pl. XI. The kitchen was in use until 1953, when the chimney was rebuilt and the room made into a dining room. Eighteenth-century English pewter plates and mid-nineteenth-century American pewter tea and coffee pots adorn the mantel.

Pl. XII. Eighteenth-century fabrics found in the house. The linen check is a bed valance; the Indian palampore dates from the first half of the eighteenth century and is used as a bed covering; the silk curtain at the right, made from a dress, once hung in front of the corner cupboard in the parlor (Pl. IV); the harrateen, which was used for upholstery, is identical in design to the crimson bed hangings of 1770 that belonged to the Saunders family of Salem and are now in the Essex Institute in Salem.

Pl. XIII. This is a fragment of the English wallpaper of 1760–1770 that was applied in the parlor over many layers of whitewash. It remained on the walls until about 1810.

The Henry Francis du Pont Winterthur Museum

BY JAMES MORTON SMITH, *Director*
CAPTIONS BY CHARLES F. HUMMEL, *Curator*

IN 1951 Henry Francis du Pont gave his house and surrounding grounds and his vast collection of American decorative arts to the Winterthur Corporation for the establishment of "a museum and arboretum for the education and enjoyment of the public."[1] Since then Winterthur has become an educational and cultural center of national significance. By preserving American interior woodwork and architecture produced between 1640 and 1840, the rooms in which people lived, and the furnishings with which they lived, Mr. du Pont created a house museum with one of the largest and richest collections of American decorative

The Henry Francis du Pont Winterthur Museum is inseparable from the carefully planned gardens, woods, and meadows that surround it. The understatement of the west facade, shown here, prepares visitors for the intimate rooms in which the fifty thousand objects in the collections are displayed. In fact, the appearance of the museum from the west is deceptive. The section of the building at the left is nine stories above the museum's main entrance and the entrance to the George and Martha Washington Wing (originally called the South Wing), which are down the hill at the right. The original three-story house of 1839–1842, now part of the Main Museum, has been engulfed by additions made over the years. The most recent was the Washington Wing, completed in 1960. The museum's abundance of windows permits visitors to enjoy beautiful views of the landscape, thus reinforcing the strong relationship of the building to its setting. *Except as noted, photographs are by courtesy of the Henry Francis du Pont Winterthur Museum.*

Winterthur's commitment to public service is manifested in the structures visible in this view from the southeast. At the left are the Main Museum (in the background) and the Washington Wing. The latter houses facilities for school tours, staff offices, and classrooms for the Winterthur Program in Early American Culture, as well as eighteen chronologically arranged period settings. The low structure next to the Washington Wing houses textile-storage facilities and offices for the mechanical-maintenance and museum-services staffs. A glass-enclosed corridor links this building with the Louise du Pont Crowninshield Research Building at the right. Completed in 1969, the Research Building houses facilities for training conservators of art objects as well as the Winterthur libraries, laboratories, and workshops devoted to the conservation of the collections. *Photograph by Gottlieb and Hilda Hampfler.*

arts. These outstanding examples of furniture and textiles, glass and ceramics, paintings and prints, and silver and other metalware are displayed in nearly two hundred alcoves, passages, and period rooms from houses great and small from New Hampshire to Georgia.

Mr. du Pont's reason for creating his extraordinary collection of collections was "to afford all those interested an opportunity to view and to study the conditions surrounding the early American home life."[2]

This portrait of Henry Francis du Pont (1880–1969) in his eighty-fifth year was completed by Aaron Shikler (b. 1922) in 1965. Mr. du Pont stands in the conservatory of the house he built for his family in 1950. The parlor in the background contains English and French antiques. The portrait captures Mr. du Pont in a pensive mood, perhaps pondering his "next" project at Winterthur, conceived in 1966 and begun in 1967—the Research Building described above, which was completed one month after his death.

As Alice Winchester observed some years ago, collecting "merely for the sake of possession gets nobody anywhere. These things are significant for what they tell more than for what they are; they are an eloquent textbook of American history. Knowledge of the domestic equipment of our ancestors is a good index to their manner of living and gives a certain insight into their way of thinking, an understanding of why they made the history they did."[3]

In order to present this domestic view of history, Winterthur trained its first guides for public tours in 1951. They serve not only as the interpreters of the collections and exhibits but also as the link between the visiting public and the curatorial, research, and teaching staffs. As S. Dillon Ripley recently observed, "museums are no longer cabinets of curiosities for the connoisseur but important instruments of public edu-

The 960-acre property of Winterthur is comprised of forests, woods, streams, meadows, and sixty intensively cultivated acres of show gardens. The design and planting of the gardens were begun before the art collections were formed. The gardens are now open to the public throughout the year. In *The Gardens of Winterthur In All Seasons*, Harold Bruce noted that "no early flowers at Winterthur are more pleasing than *Iris Reticulata*." The Royal Blue variety shown here provides evidence that March snows can be dramatic as well as traumatic. In early April, before the many varieties of deciduous trees are in leaf, colorful beds of daffodils and other narcissuses vie with magnolia blossoms for the visitor's attention. *Hampfler photographs.*

The last splurge of color before the onset of winter is the glory of the gardens in the fall, as is evident in the view of the Quarry Garden above, which shows the path leading to the museum buildings. Within the museum fresh and dried flowers and plants known to have been used by Americans between 1640 and 1840 are placed in period arrangements. They provide a human dimension to the leather-bound volumes, flute, flageolet, silver-banded snuff box, and top of a pillar-and-claw table shown in the composition below, which neatly summarizes the three major assets of Winterthur: objects, gardens, and libraries. *Top: Hampfler photograph.*

cation. Museums supplement formal instruction at all levels by giving tangible substance to abstract concepts."[4]

During the past quarter century, Winterthur has developed a complex program of museum and educational activities. In the Main Museum, which occupies the former residence of the du Pont family, period-room settings were installed continuously from 1951 to 1972. Guided tours of the Main Museum are given to those with advance reservations. Unreserved tours are given of the George and Martha Washington Wing (formerly called the South Wing), where eighteen period rooms and display areas reveal the chronological development of architectural and interior furnishing styles from the seventeenth to the nineteenth century. The Louise du Pont Crowninshield Research Building, dedicated in 1969, houses the research library and laboratories. In the Garden Pavilion, completed in 1961, are the bookstore, restaurant, reception center, and Copeland Lecture Hall, the latter added in 1964. Winterthur also owns and operates the Corbit-Sharp House and the Wilson-Warner House,

The Seventeenth Century Room is the first of the eighteen chronologically arranged period galleries and settings in the Washington Wing. This hall or kitchen from the Seth Story house, built c. 1684 in Chebacco (now Essex), Massachusetts, contains a cross section of furniture and implements available in that region during the last half of the seventeenth century. The late seventeenth-century New England white-pine stretcher-base table is set with domestic and imported wares: maple trenchers made in New England; a spoon and shaker made of horn; a pewter charger probably made by John Dolbeare of Boston between 1690 and 1710; European brass candlesticks of the last half of the seventeenth century; and, from England, a double-tined fork, latten spoon, pewter plate, brass nutcracker, and olive-green bottle. A Massachusetts maple and pine bench, or form, of 1650–1675 is drawn up to the table. It is a stretched-out version of a joint stool, such as the soft-maple New England version to the right of the fireplace. A "Brewster" and a "Carver" armchair flank the fireplace. Against the wall at the right is a leather-covered "Cromwellian"-type side chair. All three chairs were made in Massachusetts or elsewhere in New England between 1675 and 1700. The large red-oak court cupboard, an expensive case piece made for the storage of linens and the display of earthenware, silver, pewter, and other objects needed at mealtimes, was made in 1684 in Ipswich, Massachusetts, probably by Thomas Dennis (c. 1638–1706). In New England, halls or kitchens, such as the Seventeenth Century Room, were used for every human activity from cooking and eating to sleeping.

The cedar-grained and marbleized paneled fireplace wall of the William and Mary Parlor was removed from a Lincoln, Massachusetts, house built before 1700 by Thomas Goble II and renovated c. 1725 by a later owner, George Farrar. The small fielded panels and bolection molding make an appropriate backdrop for New England furniture in the William and Mary and early Queen Anne styles. To the left of the fireplace is a maple armchair attributed to John Gaines II (1677–c. 1750) of Ipswich, Massachusetts, 1711–1738. In front of it is a maple embroidery frame of 1710–1775. Beside the gateleg table, which dates from 1690–1710, is a so-called Boston side chair of 1720–1740, covered in modern leather. A European needlework imitation of a Turkey carpet, 1720–1750, covers the table, on which are a tin-glazed-earthenware punch bowl made in Bristol, England, 1720–1750, and a smaller Lambeth bowl of 1690–1720. The iron andirons are possibly from Rhode Island, 1725–1775. The hoop-shape device on the hearth in front of them is an English or American kiln for drying clay pipes, 1720–1800.

two eighteenth-century house museums in Odessa, twenty-five miles south of Wilmington.

In conjunction with the University of Delaware, the museum sponsors two of the nation's outstanding graduate programs in museum studies: the Winterthur Program in Early American Culture, a two-year interdisciplinary course in the arts and humanities leading to the master of arts degree, and the Winterthur Program in the Conservation of Artistic and Historic Objects, a three-year interdisciplinary course in the arts and sciences leading to the master of science degree.

From the beginning, Winterthur's publications office has generated books and periodicals about the collections "in order to extend the usefulness and accessibility of the Winterthur collections to a wider audience."[5]

In 1977 Winterthur's board of trustees adopted five proposals recommended by the museum's Future Directions Committee as the best means of maintaining Winterthur's position of leadership as an educational center in the field of American decorative arts and

material culture. These were to expand visits by the public, step up the publications and educational projects, institute programs to appeal to a wider audience, emphasize operating economies, and develop a five-year plan that relates long-range goals to present and potential sources of income.

The Cecil Room incorporates woodwork from a house built c. 1730 in North East, Cecil County, Maryland, and it is furnished with New England furniture and textiles of the Queen Anne period. Rhode Island examples include a rare mahogany and maple bed, 1735–1750; a maple slant-front desk with cabriole legs and pad feet, 1740–1750; a walnut armchair with rectangular splat and, next to it, a similar walnut side chair, 1725–1740; and, to the left of the bed, a walnut side chair attributed to Job Townsend (1699–1765), Newport, 1730–1750. The walnut dressing tables flanking the bed were probably made in Massachusetts, 1720–1740, as was the walnut side chair, 1740–1750, in front of the desk. The polychrome-crewel-embroidered bedspread, Boston, 1725–1750, was probably made for Thomas Hancock at the time of his marriage in 1730. American needlework is also represented by the crewelwork head-cloth, 1725–1775, showing a bird perched atop a tree, and by the New England framed needlework pictures, ranging in date from 1700 to 1760, at the left of the bed and above the desk. The crewel-embroidered window curtains are European, probably English, 1725–1775. Shown in the montage at the left are an Italian green damask valance edged with gold and green satin ribbon, 1675–1725; an Italian red silk damask, 1650–1710; and a blue silk damask, probably French, 1750–1775. The exceptional needlework purse, sewing case, and pocketbook were made by Mary Wright Alsop in Middletown, Connecticut, between 1774 and 1815. Pennsylvania needlework is represented by a picture of a large flowering tree that is related to Indian palampore designs. It is worked in silk and metallic threads, probably by Mary King, 1750–1769. The framed needlework picture of a bird in a tree, one of a pair, was worked by fourteen-year-old Sarah Wistar of Philadelphia in 1752.

One of the best examples at Winterthur of colonial America's taste for Chinese ornament is the japanned maple and white-pine high chest of drawers made by John Pimm (w. 1736–1753) of Boston for Commodore Joshua Loring between 1740 and 1750. It is displayed in the Readbourne Parlor against handsome paneling from Readbourne, built c. 1733 near Centreville, Queen Annes County, Maryland. The technique of the unknown japanner was carefully studied by the conservation staff at Winterthur. A thin coat of red lead, or vermilion, was first applied over the whole case. Black shellac was then used to give a tortoise-shell effect. Next, clear or orange shellac was applied, on top of which the japanner built up raised decoration with white lead. The raised ornament was then covered with gold leaf and the whole surface shellacked. The painted decoration was executed at this stage, and one or more finish coats of shellac were applied. Cabinetmakers working in the American Queen Anne style usually relied solely on graceful, flowing, curved lines for the effect of their furniture. However, in fashionable centers such as Boston, and especially Philadelphia, where the chairs and tea table in the parlor were made, carved ornament could be added at extra cost. The table was probably made between 1740 and 1755 for Dr. Thomas Graeme of Graeme Park, Horsham, Pennsylvania. On it is a group of English salt-glazed stoneware of 1750–1760 decorated with polychrome enamels. Although the museum's collection of paintings is small compared to its total holdings, representative works by most major American artists of the eighteenth and early nineteenth centuries are displayed. Above the fireplace is John Wollaston's (fl. 1736–1767) portrait of Mrs. Samuel Gouverneur (Experience Johnson), painted in New York between 1749 and 1752. The paneling in the Readbourne Stair Hall (right) is also from Readbourne. In the hall hangs Robert Feke's (1707–1752) portrait of Mrs. Charles Willing (Anne Shippen) of Philadelphia, completed in 1746. It was the gift of Alfred E. Bissell. Below the portrait is a mahogany side table with a Brescia-marble top made in or near Philadelphia, 1765–1775. It originally belonged to the Norris family of that city. Beside the table is a transitional walnut Chippendale side chair made in Philadelphia, 1750–1760.

The New England Kitchen (above) is based on one found in a house built c. 1740 in Oxford, Massachusetts. The flintlock musket above the fireplace was probably made in Pennsylvania, 1780–1810. The huge pair of iron andirons is English or American, 1680–1750; the iron spit and rod are probably American, 1730–1770. The English brass and iron clockwork jack, 1725–1800, provided mechanical power to turn the spit. New England windsor chairs, a New England chair table, and a cupboard made in the vicinity of Greenfield, Massachusetts, all of the eighteenth century, are examples of beautiful, practical furniture found in eighteenth- and early nineteenth-century American kitchens. Most of these objects would have been made in small craft shops like the Dominy Clock Shop and Dominy Woodworking Shop (left). The English block, or stock, knife, 1800–1830, was used by Felix Dominy (1800–1868) to prepare stock for turning on a lathe. More than eleven hundred metal- and woodworking tools used by three generations of the Dominy family between 1750 and 1850 are in the Winterthur collection.

The Marlboro Room is composed of two interiors originally in Patuxent Manor, built in 1744 in Lower Marlboro, Maryland. With the exception of a snappy Massachusetts mahogany corner table, 1730–1740, and a Virginia walnut gateleg table of c. 1725 (under the English looking glass of 1710–1720), the furniture visible here is of Philadelphia origin, of walnut or mahogany, and ranges in date from 1730 to 1780. Portraits of two Maryland brothers, painted in 1771 by Charles Willson Peale (1741–1827), also a native of Maryland, symbolize the divisions that occurred in many colonial American families during the Revolution. Colonel Edward Lloyd, his wife Elizabeth Tayloe, and their daughter Anne supported independence, while Captain Richard Bennett Lloyd was an active loyalist. The large needlework picture wrought by Sarah Warren in Boston in 1748 hangs above the fireplace in its original walnut-veneered frame. On the floor is a sumptuous hand-knotted English carpet made between 1755 and 1770, probably at Axminster or Moorfields.

A new schedule of reserved tours doubles the number of guests that can be accommodated, and the age limit has been lowered from sixteen to twelve. Special rates have been established in the Washington Wing for senior citizens and for groups. Parts of the Winterthur gardens and grounds previously closed to the public have been opened; the library's research resources have been made more accessible to the public; and student diagnostic sessions make curatorial and conservation information more widely available to the public.

The trustees specifically approved the conversion of the *Winterthur Portfolio,* an annual publication of articles about American art and cultural history, into a quarterly to be published by the University of Chicago Press. They also authorized application to the National Endowments for the Arts and Humanities for a challenge grant of $500,000 and approved a campaign to raise $1,500,000 in matching funds.

The spring and summer window hangings in the Marlboro Room are of English printed cotton made c. 1805. The pattern of Chinese pagodas and exotic foliage was originally printed in three shades of red on a mustard-yellow ground, but the ground color has completely faded away. Fortunately, a sample swatch in Winterthur's textile-study collection retains the original colors and has been used as a document for the commercial reproduction of the fabric. To preserve its great collection of antique textiles, the museum is gradually replacing those on display with reproductions of excellent quality which will enable future visitors better to understand the color schemes favored by Americans in the past. What appears to be a chest of drawers against the wall (below) is a mahogany "deception bed" made in Massachusetts, 1780-1790. On it are English tin-glazed-earthenware mugs of 1720-1750 and a Dutch tin-glazed-earthenware vase of 1680-1700. The portrait of General Walter Stewart painted between 1784 and 1788 is attributed to Robert Edge Pine (1730?-1788). To the right of the Philadelphia walnut candlestand, 1740-1750, is a walnut armchair bearing the label that William Savery (1721-1788) of that city used between 1755 and 1765. The walnut stools (in the view at the right) are from a set of four made c. 1755 which are traditionally thought to have been owned by Charles Norris of Philadelphia. They are drawn up to a Pennsylvania walnut gaming table of 1725-1750. The walnut easy chair of 1750-1770 was made in Virginia, probably in Fredericksburg, and originally belonged to the Lewis family of that town. The English looking glass also appears in the view of the room shown on the preceding page.

During the Winterthur Museum's first quarter century its expansion was financed in large part by the generosity of its founder, Henry Francis du Pont, with the assistance of admission fees and gifts from the Friends of Winterthur. During the next quarter century the museum's educational programs, which have won a national reputation, will continue to rely heavily on these traditional sources of support. To meet increasing costs, however, the museum will need major contributions from individuals, foundations, and other philanthropic agencies in order to assure the strength and vitality of its programs, which are dedicated to "the education and enjoyment of the public."

[1] Quoted in James Morton Smith, "The First Twenty-Five Years," *Henry Francis du Pont Winterthur Museum Annual Report, 1976*, p. 1.

[2] *Ibid.*

[3] ANTIQUES, May 1943, p. 207.

[4] Quoted in American Association of Museums, *Bulletin*, August 1, 1973, p. 1.

[5] E. P. Richardson, *Henry Francis du Pont Winterthur Museum Annual Report, 1962*, p. 15.

The contributions of some ethnic and religious groups to American life are preserved at Winterthur in special room installations such as this one (see also p. 1304). In 1958 woodwork and plaster ceilings from the Hehn-Kershner house, built c. 1755 in Wernersville, Berks County, Pennsylvania, were installed in space previously occupied by the Pine Kitchen. The heavy baroque-style Germanic plasterwork provides a perfect backdrop for some of the earliest Pennsylvania-German furnishings at Winterthur. At the Pennsylvania walnut dining table, 1750–1800, whose sawn, X-shape supports are the source of its modern designation as a "sawbuck" table, are three Pennsylvania walnut *brettstuhlen*, or plank chairs, 1770–1830. This type of chair was popular with the peasants of Alsace, Germany, and Switzerland from the seventeenth through the nineteenth century. The armchair in the foreground has vertical slats and a rush seat. Made between 1750 and 1800, it is related to English chairs and illustrates the interaction of the German and English immigrants who lived side-by-side in Pennsylvania. The yellow-pine chest between the windows, dated 1774, is also English in

shape, but in the German fashion it is painted red and decorated with three painted arched panels. The outer two panels contain a tulip-and-vase design, the central one five-petaled flowers. Hanging above the chest is a Philadelphia mahogany looking glass, 1762–1780, with the label of John Elliott (1713–1791), printed in English and German. To the left of the chest is a leather-covered Pennsylvania armchair which is dated 1783 on the crest rail. The pewter dial of the tall-case clock, 1765–1775, is engraved with the name of the clockmaker Jacob Graff, who worked in Lebanon County, Pennsylvania. Its walnut case combines English and German elements, and the bold, molded pediment seems appropriate to the design of the ceiling. To the right of the chest is a Pennsylvania walnut and red-pine armchair, 1750–1775, whose maker included some elements of the Chippendale style. It was discovered near Manheim, Pennsylvania, in the 1870's. Unquestionably German in design is the magnificent Lancaster County walnut *Schrank*, decorated with carving and sulphur inlay that proclaims its original ownership by Emanuel Herr of that county in 1768.

33

Against one wall of the Kershner Parlor is a Pennsylvania walnut cupboard, or dresser, 1750–1825, that is filled with examples of Pennsylvania lead-glazed red earthenware decorated with cream and green slip and scratched designs. Many of the museum's *sgraffito* (scratched) wares are signed and dated, making them important for documenting similar wares and for authenticating the homilies incised along the rims of bowls and plates. These inscriptions provide contemporary views of religion, sex, marriage, and women's roles in Pennsylvania-German society. On the top shelf, at the extreme left, is a Berks County, Pennsylvania, plate made in 1800 by Jacob Joder. Also on the top shelf, second from the right, is a plate attributed to George Hübner of Montgomery County, Pennsylvania, dated 1787, which is decorated with tulips and a peacock. John Strawn of Bucks County was the probable maker in 1797 of the plate adorned with tulips and petaled flowers (bottom shelf, extreme left). At the center of the bottom shelf is an unusual canister with the word *Tea* scratched through the slip. It was made in 1769, possibly in Wrightstown, Bucks County, Pennsylvania.

Of the hundreds of fraktur displayed throughout the museum, none is more colorful or functional than this watercolor and ink bookmark (6¾ by 4 inches) made in eastern Pennsylvania, 1790–1820, and displayed in the Kershner Parlor. The text, which is addressed to children, can be translated: "Now see, my child, the group of birds, / In spring, when they are singing / On green branches, pair by pair, / Their God a sacrifice bringing. / So sing my child, until you must journey / There in heaven's paradise."

Pewter and britannia wares retained their popularity in American secular and ecclesiastical life from earliest colonization to the Centennial celebration of 1876. The collection at Winterthur, which encompasses forms and makers from the entire period, has more pre-Revolutionary examples than any other single collection. The Pennsylvania walnut cupboard of 1750–1825 in the Kershner Kitchen holds examples of pewter and britannia wares made in New York and Philadelphia between 1710 and 1820. Among the earliest objects shown is a nineteen-inch dish by Simon Edgell (w. 1713–1742) of Philadelphia (top shelf, center). Perhaps the latest is a quart tankard by Parks Boyd (w. 1795–1819) of Philadelphia, which is second from the left on the top of the dresser. The tankard was the gift of Charles K. Davis.

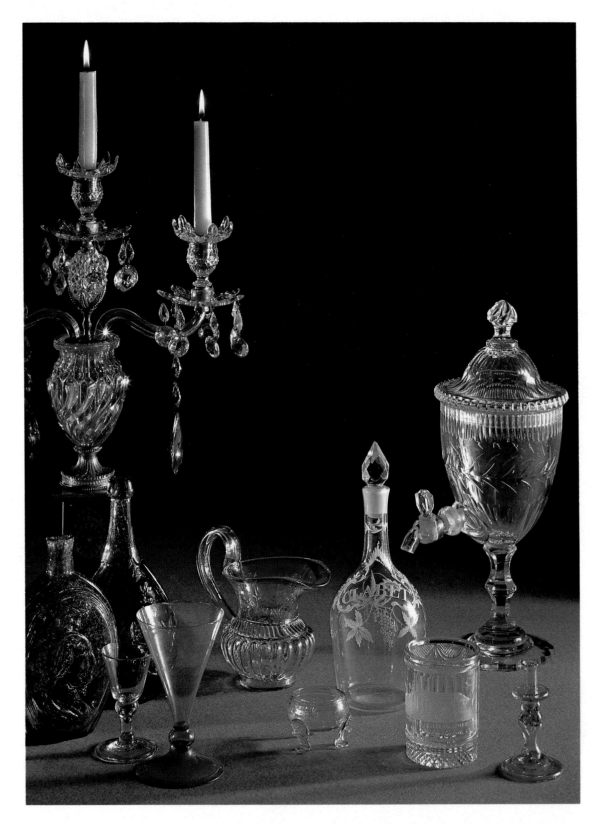

Winterthur's special collections are constantly being evaluated for authenticity and strengthened through new acquisitions. With the exception of the candelabrum, all of the objects pictured here were donated or purchased between 1973 and 1977. The flask next to the candelabrum bears a portrait of Lafayette and was made by the Coventry Glass Factory in Coventry, Connecticut, 1824–1825. The light-blue flask decorated with a likeness of Washington is a product of the Baltimore Glass Works in Baltimore, Maryland, 1825–1835. The flasks were presented by Mrs. Harry W. Lunger. The tall soda-glass drinking vessel is of the type used in colonial America. It was made on the island of Murano in Venice, 1660–1680. Next to it is a smaller English lead-glass vessel of 1700–1720. The lead-glass salt is probably from Norwich, England, 1750–1775. The enamel-decorated decanter is English, 1760–1780, and the lead-glass wine fountain is probably Irish, 1790–1800. The blown-three-mold pitcher, Maryland or Pennsylvania, 1810–1830, was the gift of Mrs. Titus Geesey. George Clark presented a pair of tumblers (one of which is shown here) which were possibly made in Bohemia and engraved in Philadelphia, 1830–1840, with views of Philadelphia landmarks. The rare blue-glass taperstick was made at the Wistarburgh Glassworks, Alloway, Salem County, New Jersey, 1739–1777, and was presented by Mr. and Mrs. Lewis Rumford II.

The vignette at the left brings together silver normally displayed in five different parts of the museum. The objects are shown in the Commons Room of the Red Lion Inn, built early in the nineteenth century in Red Lion, Delaware. The pair of candlesticks was made by Nathaniel Morse (c. 1685–1748) in Boston, 1710–1730; the coffeepot is by Jacob Hurd (1702/3–1758) of Boston, c. 1750; the two-handled covered cup was probably made by Jurian Blanck Jr. (1644–1714) in New York c. 1691; the tankard is one of a set of six bequeathed to the Third Church in Brookfield, Massachusetts, made by Paul Revere II (1735–1818) in Boston c. 1772 (see p. 1292); the porringer is by Jonathan Clarke (1706–1766) of Newport and Providence, Rhode Island, 1730–1770; the two-handled drinking bowl is probably by Henricus Boelen I (1661–1691), New York, c. 1690 (gift of Charles K. Davis); the large and magnificent covered sugar box is engraved with the date 1702 and was made by Edward Winslow (1669–1753) of Boston. Visible through the window is part of the façade of the Banister-MacKaye house built in Middletown, Rhode Island, in 1756, as installed in the Court of the Main Museum

The Queen Anne bedroom shown below is from a row house built c. 1760 by Henry Harrison in Coombs Alley, Philadelphia. The Pennsylvania walnut side chair, dressing table, and cabinet-on-frame, all dating from 1725–1755, are combined with Pennsylvania furniture made slightly later but which retains Queen Anne characteristics. The rare walnut low-post bed of 1750–1775 and a mahogany looking glass bearing the label John Elliott used between 1753 and 1762 are good examples of "unfashionable" designs which evidently continued to appeal to some craftsmen and their customers. Above the watch box hangs *A Perspective View of the Pennsylvania Hospital*, etched by James Claypoole Jr. of Philadelphia, 1761.

In and around Newport, Rhode Island, the best features of baroque design were preferred to the exuberant applied ornament of the rococo style, a fact immediately evident in the Chippendale Bedroom from the second floor of the Banister-MacKaye house. The first and second editions of Thomas Chippendale's *Director* had already been published before that house was completed in 1756. The bedroom furniture and furnishings are appropriate to a Newport merchant's country retreat. The paneling and the mahogany Rhode Island furniture rely for their effect on projecting and receding planes, the play of light and shadow, Hogarth's "line of beauty"—the cyma curve—and restrained carving of fine quality. Probably the most expensive object visible in the room would have been the unusual dwarf tall-case clock made by Thomas Claggett of Newport between 1730 and 1749. An Ushak carpet, a so-called bird rug, 1750–1800, is on the floor. Green-and-white wool damask with polychrome brocaded flowers covers the easy chair. Made in Norwich, England, 1750–1800, the fabric contrasts with the yellow silk bourette, probably French, 1725–1800, used for the valance and curtains of the bedstead. An American or European glazed-wool coverlet of the eighteenth century covers the mattress. Compare this summer treatment of the bed hangings and covers with the full winter set of European green silk taffeta hangings, 1780–1800, on the Philadelphia mahogany bedstead of 1780–1790 in the Patuxent Room which is shown at the left.

The woodwork in the Port Royal Entrance Hall is from the house of that name which Edward Stiles built in 1762 in Frankford, a suburb of Philadelphia; the wallpaper was hand painted in China between 1750 and 1775. On the floor is a wool Kurdistan carpet of the late eighteenth or early nineteenth century. The English walnut, spruce, and gilt looking glass of 1760–1770 is almost seven feet tall and is one of a pair that originally hung in the Bromfield-Phillips house on Beacon Street in Boston. It overwhelms the delicate but exuberant set of English gilt-brass wall sconces of 1750–1770. Like the mahogany Philadelphia side chairs and armchair of the same date, the sconces are in the French rococo style known then in America as the "modern" taste. The New York marble-topped "sideboard table" in the Chinese taste dates from between 1760 and 1775, and is of mahogany and mahogany veneers on a cherry frame. The walnut table near the door was made in New York, 1750–1760.

The Port Royal Parlor has been described as one of the most beautiful period-room installations in the United States. The provenance and fine quality of the woodwork called for furnishing the room with high-style Philadelphia mahogany furniture of the Chippendale period. At the far end are a high chest of drawers and matching dressing table (partly hidden by one of the sofas) made in 1769 for Michael and Miriam Gratz. The high chest's lavish and well-executed carving in the "modern" taste is difficult to top, but is certainly equaled by the slightly smaller high chest of drawers shown at the right, which stands at the other end of the room. It was produced for John or William Turner between 1765 and 1780, and was subsequently owned by the Van Pelt family. The sofas, a pair made for John Dickinson between 1775 and 1790, bear the chalk signature of John Linton, a Philadelphia upholsterer. A rare and handsome footstool, 1755–1775, made for Jacob Graff Jr. is in front of the hearth. Over the mantel hangs a view of American ships off Dover by Dominic Serrès the elder (1722–1793). On the mantel is a China Trade porcelain garniture of 1740–1760, flanked by English or Irish glass candelabra of 1780–1800. The English glass chandelier dates from 1760–1780. Behind the near sofa is a mahogany tilt-top tea table of 1760–1775 on which stand English lead-glass decanters and wine glasses that range in date from 1760 to 1780. Some of this glassware has enamel decoration by William and Mary Beilby (w. together c. 1762–1774) of Newcastle-upon-Tyne. To the right of the table is an armchair of 1765–1780 originally owned by Isaac Cooper; to the left is a side chair of 1760–1775. The Persian carpet of c. 1900, a gift from Mrs. John Ames, was woven in the Heriz region in designs often seen in earlier Kuba rugs.

This Philadelphia side chair, displayed in the Blackwell Parlor, has been attributed to the shop of Benjamin Randolph (1737/8–1791), 1760–1775. The interlaced splat, saddle-shape seat, elaborately carved seat rail, and hairy-paw feet mark this chair as an example of the best workmanship of colonial chairmakers.

The "noble savage" symbolized America to many Europeans. It is easy to understand, therefore, why a modeler at the Chelsea or Chelsea-Derby factory chose to depict America as an Indian with a quiver of arrows and one foot resting on an alligator. This figure (height 12 inches) is part of a set of the Four Continents made 1770–1775 that is displayed in the Blackwell Parlor.

This second-story room from a house on Water Street in Chester-town, Maryland, built c. 1762, provides a sympathetic background for Rhode Island, Massachusetts, and New York furniture. Set out on a mahogany breakfast table made by John Townsend (1732–1809) in Newport, 1760–1780, are transfer-printed Worcester cups and saucers, 1755–1765, and silver by Boston, Rhode Island, and New York makers: the teapot by Jacob Hurd, 1745–1755, the milk pot by Nathaniel Hurd (1729/30–1777), c. 1755, and the salver by Thomas Edwards (1701–1775), 1745–1755, all of Boston; the beaker by Samuel Casey (c. 1724–c. 1770), South Kingstown, Rhode Island, 1760–1767; and the waste bowl by William Gilbert (1746–1818), New York City, c. 1781. Attributed to John Townsend are the card table, 1770–1775; shell-carved chest of drawers, 1760–1775, and the kettle stand, 1770–1785, all of mahogany. Two Massachusetts mahogany armchairs, slip covered in English resist-dyed cotton of 1775–1800, flank the fireplace. The example at the left is attributed to Joseph Short (1771–1819) of Newburyport, Massachusetts, 1790–1795. Above the mantel hangs *The Washington Family*, an oil-on-wood-panel study painted in 1789–1790 by Edward Savage (1761–1817) and used by the artist to complete the large family group now at the National Gallery of Art. The English looking glass of 1755–1790 was presented by Martha Washington in 1794 to the wife of John E. van Alen, a congressman from Rensselaer County, New York. Under the window is a walnut footstool made in New York 1750–1760.

The "best room" of the Jerathmael Bowers house, built c. 1762 in Somerset, Massachusetts, is now in the Washington Wing and contains some of the best examples of New England Chippendale furniture at Winterthur. In front of the Boston mahogany desk-and-bookcase, 1760–1780, is a walnut and maple roundabout chair probably made in Newburyport, Massachusetts, 1760–1770. Under the portrait of Benjamin Badger, which was painted in Boston by Joseph Badger (1708–1765), 1758–1760, is a mahogany card table of 1770–1785 labeled by the Charlestown, Massachusetts, cabinetmaker Benjamin Frothingham Jr. (1734–1809). The silvered dial of the cherry tall-case clock, made 1785–1790, bears the engraved signature of Daniel Burnap (1759–1838), a clockmaker of East Windsor, Connecticut. Flanking a New York mahogany candlestand of 1760–1775 are a pair of side chairs made in Massachusetts, probably Boston, 1765–1780. The chair seats are covered with a bold English cotton furniture check of 1760–1820, a favorite eighteenth-century upholstery fabric which was also made in red, green, or brown and white.

The Chinese Parlor is devoted to evidences of the Western world's fascination with the Orient—an interest that began in the seventeenth century and remains undiminished today. Although direct trade between America and China was not established until 1784, objects made in the Orient or in the "Chinese taste" were available earlier to colonial Americans by way of Holland, England, and France. The room is dominated by the wallpaper, hand painted in China 1770–1780, which depicts life in a Chinese village. The furniture, primarily from Philadelphia but including examples from Massachusetts, New York, Rhode Island, and South Carolina, reflects elements of the "Gothic, Chinese and modern taste" popularized by Thomas Chippendale. On the shelves of the cupboard at the right of the fireplace is a group of *encre de chine* porcelains decorated for the Western market between 1730 and 1770. Additional examples are on the tea table at one end of the sofa. A fine Ch'ien Lung (1736–1795) porcelain tureen in the form of a goose almost blends into the wallpaper from its perch atop the side table at the right. The Persian Kurdistan carpet, 1770–1800, is flanked by Chinese Turkestan silk carpets of 1830–1870. By the early nineteenth century American merchantmen were the most successful competitors of the British East India Company for supremacy in the China Trade. Symbolic of that competition is the fine China Trade porcelain covered jug of c. 1805 (height 11 inches) shown at the right, which bears a likeness of Captain Stephen Decatur Sr. taken from a Saint-Mémin engraving of 1802.

The jug which appears in this grouping of China Trade porcelain is very similar to the one illustrated on the preceding page. This example bears a copy of David Edwin's (1776–1841) engraving of George Washington, and was given between 1810 and 1820 to Edward Tilghman by his uncle Benjamin Chew Wilcocks, a Philadelphia merchant and the American consul at Canton. The leaf-shape dish bears a view of the *Philadelphia*, which was owned by the Union Line and sailed the Chesapeake Bay between 1816 and 1841. The other three examples of Chinese porcelains made for the American market all date between 1790 and 1830. They are decorated respectively with the eagle from the great seal of the United States, an ermine mantle enclosing initials, and a Chinese landscape.

The Chinese porcelain cup and saucers, made in 1761 or later, are decorated with illustrations from a book of anatomy. The European or American mahogany medicine chest, 1790–1825, is fitted with glass bottles and a glass mortar and pestle.

The dining room used by Mr. and Mrs. Henry Francis du Pont from 1932 to 1951 contains a set of twelve New York mahogany arm and side chairs originally owned by the French-born Victor Marie du Pont. He may have purchased them while he was a member of the French legation in the United States in 1787 and between 1791 and 1793, but it seems more likely that he acquired them for his dining room after his family immigrated to America early in 1800. The legs of the Baltimore dining table of c. 1800 are inlaid with eagles. The ale glasses on the table are engraved with the seal of the Order of the Cincinnati. Flanking the fireplace are cupboards filled with China Trade porcelain decorated with variations of the great seal of the United States. Above the fireplace hangs Gilbert Stuart's (1755–1828) oil portrait of George Washington of 1795–1796. On the wall opposite (shown at the right) hangs Benjamin West's (1738–1820) unfinished oil sketch of 1782–1784 depicting the American commissioners (seated) John Adams, Benjamin Franklin, William Temple Franklin, and (standing) John Jay and Henry Laurens, who were negotiating the preliminary peace treaty with England in 1782. Below the painting is a New York sideboard of 1795–1805 on which stands a set of tankards made c. 1772 by Paul Revere II.

Throughout the nineteenth century Americans used Greek and Roman sources as models for their thought, conduct, and works of art. The figure in the foreground of this view of the Hall of Statues, perhaps a representation of Ceres, and the figure holding a dove at the left, are excellent examples of the wood sculpture produced in Massachusetts between 1800 and 1840. The motto on the 1800–1820 sign of B. Little, a Hudson River valley coach painter, reads, *Plenty and Peace throughout the World.* A print almost identical to the composition painted on the sign was published in London in 1802. The Pennsylvania wood sculptor of the group of figures in the corner called on all popular symbols for his representation of Liberty crowning George Washington. Made between 1840 and 1870, possibly in Philadelphia, the group appeared in an engraving in McElroy's Philadelphia *Directory* of 1856 with the motto *Encourage American Arts.* Long after the American Revolution, the eagle, Liberty, and George Washington as a noble Roman exercised a strong appeal for citizens like *K. Wood,* who was captured in a head-and-shoulders portrait by the sculptor James Fell of New York State in 1824.

The interior woodwork and French wall-paper of the Federal Parlor were in a 1794–1796 wing of the Phelps-Hatheway house in Suffield, Connecticut. The cherry desk-and-bookcase was made in Connecticut or Rhode Island, 1790–1810. The cherry side chairs by the desk are from a set of six in the room that were made by Samuel Kneeland and Lemuel Adams (w. together 1792–1796) in Hartford in 1793. Other furniture in the room was made in Massachusetts, New York, and Rhode Island.

The Baltimore Drawing Room incorporates interior elements from a Philadelphia house built c. 1812 by the famous maker of composition ornament Robert Welford. With three exceptions the furniture in the room was made in Baltimore or Philadelphia. The pembroke table bearing a silver service by Joseph Richardson Jr. (1752–1831), c. 1790, and the side chair at the desk were probably made in South Carolina, 1790–1800; and the lolling chair of c. 1805 near the fireplace bears the label of Lemuel Churchill (w. 1805–c. 1828) of Boston.

The architectural elements that make up the Phyfe Room (above and right) were removed from Moses Rogers' house at 7 State Street, New York City, which was remodeled in 1806. The four side chairs and possibly the two armchairs are believed to be from one of two sets of mahogany chairs Duncan Phyfe (1768–1854) made in 1807 for William Bayard, who lived at 6 State Street in New York. The only labeled example of Phyfe's furniture at Winterthur is a square worktable with canted corners and an inset marble top made c. 1815. It is to the left of the pianoforte made by John Geib Jr. (w. 1815–1822) and dated 1818. In front of the scroll-back cane sofa, probably made in Phyfe's shop between 1805 and 1810, is a New York mahogany sofa table of 1810–1820. On it are a flageolet and a boxwood flute, both made between 1820 and 1832 by E. Riley of 29 Chatham Street, New York. The elaborate painted and gilded overmantel glass in the view at the right was made in New York City or Albany c. 1805, and was originally owned by Governor Joseph C. Yates and his wife, of Albany, New York. The French ormolu clock on the mantel was a wedding present to Pierre Samuel du Pont and Anne Alexandrine de Montchanin in 1766. Also of French origin are the two Aubusson-type rugs used in this room and alternated with the seasons. The one shown at the right was made between 1825 and 1850 and was the gift of Mrs. Henry R. Silliman. The tapestry-weave example illustrated above dates from 1770–1800.

Most visitors to Winterthur are impressed by the beauty, elegance, and superb craftsmanship embodied in the modern freestanding staircase in the Montmorenci Stair Hall. Its design was inspired by a stair, now destroyed, which was in Montmorenci, built c. 1822 in Shocco Springs, near Warrenton, North Carolina. In 1935 and 1936 Henry Francis du Pont combined elements from that house and placed them within an existing stairwell at Winterthur. The settee, side chairs, and worktable of mahogany and figured birch veneers are attributed to the Boston shop of John and/or Thomas Seymour, c. 1805. The card table at the right of the staircase, a bequest from Mrs. Francis B. Crowninshield, is also of mahogany and figured birch veneers, and it too was made in Boston, c. 1810.

The Miniature Stair Hall is furnished with diminutive ceramics, silver, utensils, hooked rugs, dolls, lighting devices, and furniture. In a drawer of the mahogany sideboard, possibly made in Concord, Massachusetts, 1790–1810, is a set of silver spoons, probably from Hudson, New York, 1840–1848. A miniature tea service sits on a New England mahogany candlestand of 1760–1780; framed in the window is a walnut high chest of drawers complete with finials and pendant drops made in Connecticut, 1750–1780.

In 1971 the Friends of Winterthur provided a grant that made possible the installation in the following year of the Georgia Dining Room (left) as a memorial to Henry Francis du Pont, who had died in 1969. The interior is that of the back parlor, originally used as a dining room, from the Samuel Rockwell mansion, built c. 1837 in Milledgeville, Georgia. It occupies the last space available for a room installation in the present museum. The mahogany extension dining table of 1810–1819 bears the stamp of the French *émigré* cabinetmaker Charles-Honoré Lannuier (w.c. 1803–1819) and is traditionally thought to have belonged to John Macpherson Berrien, who lived in Georgia. Lannuier is known to have shipped furniture to the port of Savannah. The table is set with part of a sixty-four-piece dessert service that President James Monroe ordered for the White House in 1817 from the Paris firm of Pierre Louis Dagoty and Edouard Honoré. Other pieces from that service are shown in the photograph at the bottom of the page. The medallions in the borders contain emblems of agriculture, art, commerce, science, and war. Around the Lannuier table are four of a set of six painted maple klismos-type side chairs made in New York or Philadelphia, 1810–1825. They were a gift of the heirs of F. Donaldson

Brown. A rare ingrain, or Scotch, carpet from the British Isles, 1820–1840, covers the floor. The portraits of Benjamin and Mary Hunter Tevis were painted in Philadelphia in 1822 and 1827, respectively, by Thomas Sully (1783–1872). The pair of candlesticks on the Lannuier table was made by Simon Chaudron and Anthony Rasch in Philadelphia between 1809 and 1812 and demonstrates direct French influence on American silver design. On the sideboard, which is attributed to Anthony G. Quervelle (fl. 1825–1849), Philadelphia, 1825–1835, is a silver covered ewer, 1812–1820, by the great Philadelphia firm of Fletcher and Gardiner (1808–1827). Their Baltimore rival, Samuel Kirk (1793—1872), was responsible in 1828 for the six-piece coffee and tea service on the table at the left. That table is half of a dining table made in New York or Philadelphia, 1820–1840. The other section of the table is visible through the doorway in the Empire Vestibule. Also in the Vestibule is the handsome grained, gilt-stenciled, ash and cherry Grecian couch shown below. It was made in New York, 1820–1835, and is a recent addition to the collection. Fellows of the Winterthur Program in Early American Culture were responsible for the research that established the correct upholstery for the couch.

The Empire Parlor (left), installed and first furnished in 1940 by Henry Francis du Pont, contains architectural elements from the General Rufus King house, built c. 1839 in Albany, New York. It is one of a group of rooms that will be changed as little as possible so that cultural historians in the future can study Mr. du Pont's approach to period-room installation. The New York furniture in the room includes klismos-type side chairs of 1815–1830, and a lute- or scroll-back side chair of 1825–1840 near a gilt-stenciled worktable made by Roswell A. Hubbard, 1834–1836. The New York center table of 1815–1825 in the foreground has a plaster top with a painted depiction of the packet *Cornwallis* capturing the pirate ship *Gloria*. The New York center table in the background, made 1820–1830, is set with part of a forty-three-piece porcelain coffee and tea service decorated in the "French taste," which was made in Philadelphia, 1825–1838, by William E. Tucker (1800–1832), or successors to his firm. The service was the gift of Philip Hammerslough. Two porcelain pitchers made by the same company between 1832 and 1836 are placed on the base of a New York mahogany and marble pier table, one of a pair, 1820–1830. An English or American girandole looking glass, 1810–1820, hangs above an ormolu mantel clock designed by Dubuc of Paris, 1800–1819, as a tribute to George Washington. French tapestry-woven Aubusson-type carpets of 1800–1830 cover the floor. The bronze, ormolu, and glass chandelier, 1825–1850, could have been made in France or the United States.

The furnishings of the Empire Hall in the Washington Wing include an ebonized-wood and gilt-stenciled marble-topped New York pier table of 1820 to 1835 owned by the Sleight family of Sag Harbor; a pair of New England gilded looking glasses, 1815–1825, with a tradition of ownership by Jonathan Hatch Hubbard, a Vermont Supreme Court justice; and a New England desk veneered with mahogany and bird's-eye maple, c. 1820, which is said to have been used in the Concord, New Hampshire, statehouse. The unidentified gentleman painted by Samuel Waldo and William Jewett (w. together 1820–1854) in New York in 1823 was the gift of Mr. and Mrs. Orrin W. June.

Long before Walter Gropius, Mies van der Rohe, Frank Lloyd Wright, and others preached that less is more and that form follows function, members of the United Society of Believers in Christ's Second Appearing in communities from Maine to Kentucky distilled the design of buildings and objects to bare essentials while permitting their ideals, spirituality, and love of beauty to be reflected in their products. The Shaker Dwelling Room is one of three Shaker exhibits installed at Winterthur in 1962. It incorporates woodwork from a large stone dwelling house built in the Enfield, New Hampshire, community early in the nineteenth century. The paint on the floorboards, peg rail, and built-in wall storage units approximates the original colors. In the foreground is a striped-maple rocking side chair, 1820–1870, used by the eldress of the South Family at the Niskeyuna community, Watervliet,

New York. It is drawn up to a ten-foot-long cherry and maple communal dining table probably produced in the New Lebanon, New York, community. The painted bedstead was made in the Hancock Shaker community, Pittsfield, Massachusetts, 1830–1850, and the cherry candlestand, at Enfield, Connecticut, 1790–1830. The cast-iron stove was made in the New Lebanon, New York, community, 1800–1900. Attached to the back of the stove is a rod from which hang a shovel and tongs, also from New Lebanon. The fireplace tools were the gift of Helen, Margaret, and Pauline Brown. The stovepipe was designed and installed according to photographs of similar installations in Shaker dwelling houses. The birch and maple rocking armchair was probably made in the New Lebanon community. It was given by the Halcyon Foundation.

Winterthur's large collections permit comparisons of objects by form, materials, decoration, date, design, or in almost any combination of these desired. Part of the collection of toleware is displayed on painted shelves of 1750 to 1825 in Red Lion Hall and in the arrangement at the right. These tin-plated sheet-iron bread trays, boxes, chambersticks, covered sugar bowls, cups, coffee or tea pots, tumblers, pitchers, and tea caddies were made in New England and Pennsylvania between 1820 and 1860 and were often sold by itinerant peddlers. Also visible through the entranceway to Red Lion Hall are a painted windsor side chair made in the mid-Atlantic states, 1775–1795, and a painted hexagonal table made of pine and maple in Pennsylvania, 1750–1775. Completing this view of utilitarian, popular objects is a handsome oval hooked rug made in New England c. 1850.

The cobblestoned Court is enclosed by four different full-scale architectural facades, and evokes the atmosphere of an early nineteenth-century urban courtyard or town square. This view shows the reconstructed façade of a typical Connecticut River valley house of c. 1750. The massive pedimented doorway is from the Dwight-Barnard (later Bliss) house, built in the mid-eighteenth century in Springfield, Massachusetts. A corner of the rusticated imitation-sandstone front of the Banister-MacKaye house is visible at the right. At the left is the brick exterior of the Red Lion Inn. Indicative of the continuous refinement of the installations at Winterthur is the fact that the tavern sign of J. Procter, 1800-1840, will be replaced by the original signboard from the Red Lion Inn, a recent gift from the New Castle Historical Society. Nearly thirty different examples of windsor furniture are displayed in the Court. By the octagonal maple and pine music or reading stand, American, 1790-1830, are two braced fan-back windsor armchairs, probably Pennsylvania or the mid-Atlantic states, 1770-1800. In the foreground is a New England braced fan-back armchair of the same date. The settee in the background was made in Philadelphia or Baltimore, and is branded I MILLER twice under the seat; the settee in front of the Red Lion Inn was probably made in Pennsylvania. Both date from between 1770 and 1800.

Middleton Place

BY SARAH LYTLE, *Director, Middleton Place Foundation*

Pl. I. Looking west across the Ashley River to Middleton Place, near Charleston, South Carolina. Middleton Place House (Pl. II) is in the shadow at the left of center. The rice-mill pond extending into the trees at the left empties into the butterfly lakes at the foot of the terraces, which in turn flood the rice field to the right of the lakes. *Photograph by Gene Gibbs.*

HENRY MIDDLETON (1717–1784) acquired the plantation now called Middleton Place by marriage to Mary Williams in 1741. The three-story main house, high on a bluff overlooking the Ashley River, was apparently not architecturally exceptional.[1] However, by 1755 Middleton had added a wing to the south containing offices and a laundry on the ground floor and extra sleeping quarters for visiting gentlemen on the second floor, and a wing to the north in which the ground floor was a conservatory and the second floor housed a library and an art gallery. At the same time, Middleton began to shape the extraordinary gardens that were as celebrated a feature of the plantation in the mid-eighteenth century as they are today.

Contouring the bluff to create the sweeping ripples of terraced lawns, symmetrical butterfly lakes, and formal gardens (see Pl. I) required the labor of some one hundred men for a period of nearly ten years. One of the most important aspects of the garden is the inventive use of water. An ingenious system of

Fig. 1. Plan of Middleton Place.

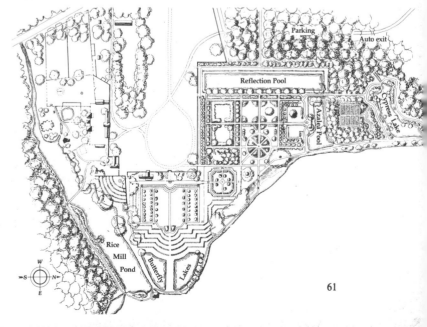

61

Pl. II. What is today Middleton Place House is actually the south wing, completed in 1755, that Henry Middleton (1717–1784) added to the house he acquired from his father-in-law, John Williams, on his marriage to Mary Williams in 1741. Middleton added a matching wing to the north of the main house at the same time. As the part of the house least damaged by Union troops during the Civil War, the south wing was remodeled and enlarged by 1870 to serve as the Middleton family's residence. *Photograph by R. Alan Powell.*

ponds and lakes, at once ornamental and utilitarian, drains the swamp after providing power for the small rice mill and flooding a series of riverside rice fields.

Eighteenth-century visitors would most often have come to Middleton Place by boat from Charleston, which explains the impressive river approach to the property. Those who arrived by the Ashley River Road entered through gates a quarter of a mile from the house and passed by lawns kept closely cropped by sheep invisibly fenced by ha-has.[2] It is more like the approach to an English country manor than to the typical Southern plantation house shaded by live oaks hung with Spanish moss.

Henry Middleton, although born near Charleston, was of English descent. He served in a number of important political positions in the colony of South Carolina and in 1774 he was elected a delegate from South Carolina to the first Continental Congress, of which he was briefly president.[3]

Both of Henry Middleton's sons, Arthur (1742–1787) and Thomas (1753–1797), went to school in England, and from 1768 to 1771 Arthur and his wife Mary Izard traveled in Europe. During that time Arthur studied the "fine arts at Rome and perfected his taste in literature, music and painting."[4] Before their departure from London for Charleston in 1771 Middleton commissioned Benjamin West to paint his family (Pl. V). In 1775 Arthur Middleton was elected

Pl. III. The terraces leading from the river to the parterre are cut into a natural hillside. The house is on one of the highest—and thus, some supposed, one of the healthiest—points in the Charleston region. *Photograph by Charles H. P. Duell.*

Pl. IV. The main room in the house contains portraits of the four generations of the Middleton family who lived there from 1741 until the Civil War. Above the table hangs Benjamin West's portrait of Arthur and Mary Izard Middleton and their son Henry (Pl. V). Next to the window is a likeness of Williams Middleton (1809–1883). The table beneath the West portrait is described in Pls. VIII and IX; the chairs flanking it, in Pl. VII. *Except as noted, photographs are by N. Jane Iseley.*

Fig. 2. Ruins of the Middleton Place plantation house after it was burned by Union troops on February 22, 1865. The photograph, half of a stereopticon view, dates from c. 1866. *Middleton Place Foundation.*

Pl. V. Portrait of Arthur (1742–1787) and Mary Izard Middleton (1747–1814) and their son Henry (1770–1846) by Benjamin West (1738–1820), London, 1771. Oil on canvas, 49½ by 71¾ inches. Later generations of Middletons affectionately referred to this picture as "the Holy Family." West had painted a portrait of Arthur Middleton (now at Middleton Place) when the latter was a student at St. John's College, Cambridge University (1761–1763). He also executed likenesses of Arthur's father, Henry, c. 1770 (now at Middleton Place), and of Arthur's brother, Thomas (1753–1797); the latter is in the Gibbes Art Gallery in Charleston. *Collection of Dr. Henry Middleton Drinker, on loan to Middleton Place Foundation.*

Pl. VI. Detail of a copy on silk of the Declaration of Independence by Benjamin Owen Tyler (b. 1789), 1818, showing Arthur Middleton's signature. Tyler called himself a "professor of penmanship" on the bottom of the document.

to succeed his father as South Carolina's delegate to the Continental Congress, and in that capacity he became one of the signers of the Declaration of Independence (see Pl. VI).[5]

Arthur's eldest son, Henry (1770–1846), enjoyed an active career in government service. His considerable fortune enabled him to be a member of the state legislature, governor of South Carolina (1810–1812), and a United States congressman (1815–1819). From 1820 to 1830 he and his family lived in St. Petersburg, where Henry was United States minister plenipotentiary to the Russian court.[6] Even though he was much away from Middleton Place Henry Middleton did not

Pl. VII. Side chair, one of a pair in the main room (see Pl. IV), American, possibly Southern, c. 1770. Mahogany; height 38¼, width 24, depth 17¾ inches. The chairs were probably owned by Daniel Huger (1741–1799) of Charleston.

neglect it, and he greatly embellished and expanded the gardens. In 1840 a visitor wrote that Middleton Place

is substantial and durable as ever and will probably endure, like the venerable oaks, which shade the adjacent grounds, until the day of final doom . . . the interior of the house is elegantly furnished, and the walls are decorated with numerous paintings, portraits, and historical fancy pieces, by the great masters of the divine art. . . . Several of the paintings exhibit scenes in St. Petersburg, where Mr. Middleton, so long and so worthily, represented as Ambassador to Russia, the interests and the honor of our great Republic.[7]

Pl. VIII. Table attributed to Thomas Elfe (1719–1775), Charleston c. 1770. Mahogany; height 27⅞, width (open) 42½, depth 24 inches. The table, which stands in the main room (Pl. IV), is very similar to another table attributed to Elfe, in the Heyward-Washington House in Charleston. The "figure-eight" motif in the skirt (Pl. IX) is typical of Elfe's work.

Pl. IX. Detail of the skirt on the table shown in Pl. VIII.

Pl. X. The music room is furnished to reflect the travels and taste of Governor Henry Middleton (1770–1846). He acquired the portrait of Czar Nicholas I (on the wall at the right) while serving in the 1820's as United States minister plenipotentiary to the Russian court in St. Petersburg. The studies of two women flanking the door are early nineteenth-century French works after Jean-Baptiste Greuze. The portrait of Mme Récamier at the left is illustrated in Pl. XIII. The suite of furniture was probably made in Philadelphia c. 1815 (see also Pl. XI). The late eighteenth-century flute on the chair in front of the music stand was made in London by T. Cahusac. The clock on the pier table is illustrated in Pl. XII. The Aubusson rug dates from the early nineteenth century.

Pl. XI. Pedestal table, probably Philadelphia, c. 1815. Mahogany and tulip poplar, marble top, gilt stenciled decoration. Height 29½; diameter of top, 38 inches. The table is part of the suite of furniture in the music room (Pl. X).

Williams Middleton (1809–1883) took over the management of Middleton Place on the death of his father, Henry, in 1846; but Williams, his wife, Susan Pringle Smith, and their two children were forced to flee Charleston when Union troops advanced on the city in 1865. Because Williams Middleton had signed the Ordinance of Secession and had contributed hundreds of thousands of dollars to the Southern cause, his property was a natural target for the Union

Pl. XII. The elaborate gold and brass clock in the music room (Pl. X) was made c. 1760 by Leroy et Fils of Paris. At twelve o'clock the grill automatically opens to reveal the monk, who pulls a rope to ring the hour.

Pl. XIII. Portrait of Mme Récamier by M. Guerin after the portrait by François Pascal Simon, baron Gérard, early nineteenth century. Oil on porcelain, 14½ by 9⅝ inches. The portrait was probably commissioned by John Izard Middleton (1785–1849), the youngest son of Arthur and Mary Izard Middleton. John Izard Middleton, an artist and scholar who lived most of his life in Paris and Rome, frequented the salons of Mme Récamier and Mme de Stael during the first decade of the nineteenth century.

Pl. XIV. The dining room looks west onto the greensward. On the wall at the left hangs a view of the Bay of Naples painted by an Italian artist in the early nineteenth century. It was one of three paintings stolen from the house in 1865 by a Union officer, who returned them ten years later to Williams Middleton. The center portion of the mahogany banqueting table was found in a barn on the plantation early in this century. It is English of the late eighteenth century; the ends are reproductions. On the table is French soft-paste porcelain of the early nineteenth century. The epergne is shown in Pl. XV. Judging from contemporary prints, elaborate bird cages such as the one between the windows were common in Charleston houses in the late eighteenth century.

Pl. XV. Arthur Middleton purchased the silver epergne in London in 1771. It was made by Francis Butty and Nicholas Dumee (in partnership c. 1761–1773). The bottom of each basket is chased with the Middleton coat of arms.

troops. On February 22, 1865, after ransacking the abandoned plantation and enjoying a fine dinner in the house, Union officers set fire to Middleton Place. Only the gutted south wing and a very few of the family's possessions survived the fire (see Fig. 2).[8]

By 1870 the south wing had been restored as the Middletons' residence (Pl. II), but there were grim periods for the descendants of the first Henry Middleton during Reconstruction,[9] the destructive earthquake of 1886, World War I, and the Depression. When J. J. Pringle Smith, a descendant of Henry Middleton, and his wife, Heningham Ellett, came to Middleton Place in 1916 they undertook a complete restoration of the gardens (which they opened to the

Pl. XVI. Knife box, English, c. 1790. Mahogany inlaid with satinwood; height 15 inches.

Pl. XVII. The bed hangings, window curtains, and upholstery in the winter bedroom are made from a reproduction of a heavy French eighteenth-century toile. The mahogany bed was made in Charleston c. 1800. Such beds are often referred to as rice-post beds because of the rice motif carved on the footposts (see Pl. XVIII). The headboard is removable. The mahogany clothespress, made in Charleston in the late eighteenth century, contains clothes made in London between about 1750 and 1775 for Henry and Arthur Middleton.

Pl. XVIII. The early nineteenth-century South Carolina fall-front desk in the winter bedroom (Pl. XVII) is of mahogany inlaid with holly. The clock was made in London c. 1780. Above it hangs an engraving of Diana and Actaeon published in London c. 1764.

Pl. XIX. The miniature of George Washington (oil on porcelain, 7⅜ by 2⅞ inches) was painted by William R. Birch (1755–1834) in 1797. In front of it are an early medal of the Society of the Cincinnati, a gold shoe buckle that belonged to Arthur Middleton, and a gold patch box that belonged to his wife, Mary.

public) and the south wing, which is all that remains of the house to this day. Their grandson Charles H. P. Duell opened the stable yards to the public in 1970 to give visitors an idea of the daily routine of plantation life. In 1975 he opened the house itself to the public. It is operated by the Middleton Place Foundation, a nonprofit public trust, and serves as the repository for the many paintings, objects, books, and documents contributed by members of the Middleton family from as far away as Great Britain and Arizona.

Middleton Place is a National Historic Landmark. The small professional staff that administers it engages in research programs as diverse as archaeological excavations and cataloguing and microfilming manuscripts. Much valuable information has been lost as a result of fire, neglect, and the climate of the lowlands, but there is an enormous commitment to continue to assemble the remaining evidence of what life was once like at Middleton Place.

Pl. XX. The summer bedroom is furnished to show how those living on a South Carolina plantation coped with the summer heat. Rush matting was laid on the floor; the bed, here a mahogany rice-post bed made in Charleston c. 1800, was moved to the middle of the room, and the headboard removed to allow better air circulation; and the heavy winter window and bed hangings were replaced with mosquito netting and light dimity. The engravings of flowers after Baptiste were published in the mid-eighteenth century. See also Pl. XXI.

Pl. XXII. On the shelves of this English mahogany desk-and-bookcase, c. 1790, are some of the books on gardening that belonged to the Middleton family. The family library has been greatly reduced but it is still strong in volumes on ornamental horticulture, landscape architecture, local, Southern, and natural history.

Pl. XXI. The summer bedroom overlooks the parterre and the Ashley River. The pair of English mahogany side chairs of c. 1790 were originally at Weehaw, a Middleton family plantation, near Georgetown, South Carolina.

Pl. **XXIII.** This silver tankard was made in London in 1743 by Richard Gurney and Thomas Cooke II (in partnership 1721–1773), and is engraved with the Middleton coat of arms.

Pl. **XXIV.** Portrait of Septima Sexta Middleton Rutledge (1783–1865) by Edward Marchant (1806–1887), c. 1825. Oil on canvas, 29¼ by 24½ inches. As her name implies, the sitter was the seventh child and sixth daughter of Arthur and Mary Izard Middleton. In 1799 she married her first cousin Henry Middleton Rutledge (1775–1844), who was the son of Henrietta Middleton and Edward Rutledge, a signer of the Declaration of Independence. Septima and Henry Rutledge settled on land granted by the United States government to his father in Nashville, Tennessee.

Pl. **XXV.** Pair of andirons, possibly Charleston, c. 1760. Bell metal; height 27 inches. They belonged to Oliver Hering Middleton (1798–1892), a son of Governor Henry Middleton.

Pl. XXVI. The stable yard and its buildings were designed and constructed in the 1930's by Bancel Lafarge after he had made a study of eighteenth-century outbuildings in South Carolina and the West Indies.

Pl. XXVII. The collection of nineteenth-century horse-drawn vehicles at Middleton Place includes a landaulet, in the foreground; a brougham; and a three-seated surrey. *Powell photograph.*

Pl. XXVIII. These wagon wheels are propped against a wall of the carpenter's shop. *Powell photograph.*

Pl. XXIX. Mallard and wood ducks feed in the shallow rice-mill pond near the bridge which connects the azalea hillside (see Pl. XLII) with the stable yard.

Pl. XXX. Camelias were introduced to the Middleton Place gardens late in the eighteenth century, probably by Governor Henry Middleton, who may have been given them by his friend the French botanist André Michaux (1746–1802).

Pl. XXXI. The reflection pool forms the western boundary of the formal garden. Eighteenth-century landscape designers often recommended placing swans in formal gardens.

Pl. XXXIII. In contrast to the formal gardens and in keeping with nineteenth-century romantic inclinations is the azalea pool garden created in the mid-nineteenth century, where narrow paths wind beside a pond and through woods informally planted with azaleas.

Pl. XXXII. *Wood Nymph*, by Johann Gottfried Schadow (1764–1850), German, c. 1810. Height 46 inches. This marble figure is the sole survivor of the many statues that once adorned the gardens. The others were destroyed during the Revolution and Civil War. This statue survived only because in 1865 Williams Middleton, then owner of Middleton Place, buried it in the garden before Union troops sacked the plantation.

Pl. **XXXIV.** Royal mute swans in one of the butterfly lakes.

Pls. **XXXV, XXXVI.** Michaux introduced crepe myrtle, an Oriental, smooth-barked flowering tree, to South Carolina c. 1787. This is one of the largest known specimens.

Pl. **XXXVII.** View from the bridge over the rice-mill pond in the late afternoon.

Pl. XXXVIII. Black swans swim in the rice-mill pond.

Pl. XXXIX. Pampas grass grows in abundance on the banks of the rice field and the rice-mill pond.

Pl. XL. Beyond the stone urn are one of the butterfly lakes, the rice mill, and part of the rice-mill pond. *Duell photograph.*

[1] The only plan of the house known was drawn by a journeyman architect in 1864 for Williams Middleton, who intended to make additions to the house. It is in the collection of Middleton Place Foundation.

[2] Langdon Cheves, "Middleton of South Carolina," *South Carolina Historical and Genealogical Magazine*, vol. 1 (July 1900), pp. 253-254.

[3] *Ibid.*

[4] *Ibid.*, p. 253.

[5] *Ibid.*, p. 245.

[6] *Ibid.*

[7] *Courier*, Charleston, March 7, 1840.

[8] Dr. Henry O. Marcy witnessed the fire and recorded his account in his diary, a photocopy of which is at Middleton Place.

[9] Williams Middleton's letters, in the collection at Middleton Place, are revealing about the fate of the plantation after the Civil War.

Pl. XLII. Azaleas were introduced to the garden in the middle of the nineteenth century (see Pl. **XXXIII**) and were planted in profusion in the 1930's on the hillside along the southern bank of the rice-mill pond.

Pl. XLI. The cypress lake was created out of a swamp in this century to separate the gardens from the woods to the north.

Pl. XLIV. Jack-in-the-pulpit is one of the many species of wild flowers that grow near the cypress lake.

Pl. XLIII. The Southern bald cypress "breathes" through spiky protrusions called knees.

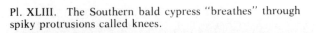

Historic houses owned by the Essex Institute in Salem, Massachusetts

BY GERALD W. R. WARD, *Assistant curator,*
Garvan and Related Collections of
American Art, Yale University Art Gallery
AND BARBARA M. WARD *Research assistant*

Pl. I. John Ward House (built after 1684) in its present location on the grounds of the Essex Institute. As it stands now, the house is a jumble of features dating from the original construction and from the period of the restoration by George Francis Dow (1868-1936) in this century. The massive gables, which had been removed in the eighteenth century, were reconstructed on the basis of interior evidence. Dow installed reproduction casement windows based on examples in the collection of the Essex Institute after finding part of one casement window within the walls of the house. The central chimney stack was rebuilt to resemble other known seventeenth-century New England examples. *Except as noted, photographs are by Helga Photo Studio.*

THE ESSEX Historical Society (incorporated 1821) and the Essex County Natural History Society (incorporated 1836) merged in 1848 to form the Essex Institute, dedicated to preserving "authentic memorials" of the county's civil history.[1] The Institute has always interpreted this responsibility to include the preservation of Salem's "ancient" structures—as early as 1865 it acquired a small building then thought to be Salem's original 1629 meetinghouse—and today it maintains a group of seven historic houses, six of which are open to the public. Beginning with the relocation in 1910 and subsequent restoration of the John Ward House (built after 1684), the Institute has preserved distinguished examples of local domestic architecture. The Peirce-Nichols (probably built 1782, remodeled 1801), Assembly (built 1782, remodeled 1796-1798), and Gardner-Pingree (built

1804-1805) houses document each phase of the career of Samuel McIntire, while the Crowninshield-Bentley House (built 1727-1729 with later eighteenth-century additions) illustrates stylistic changes throughout the eighteenth century. The Andrew-Safford House (built 1818-1819) is evidence of the aspirations of local merchants during Salem's last years as a thriving port city. The Institute's museum and library are themselves housed in two important nineteenth-century buildings: Plummer Hall (built in 1857 for the Salem Atheneum) and the John Tucker Daland House (the Institute's seventh historic house, built in 1851 to the design of Gridley J. F. Bryant [1816-1899]). In addition, the museum maintains a large collection of architectural fragments that includes examples of ornaments carved by McIntire and the notable doorway of the Thomas Poynton Ives house (built 1740) with its beautifully carved pineapple finial, as well as doorways from other Salem houses. A large group of McIntire drawings and a superb collection of early photographs, prints, and drawings add to the strength of the Institute's architectural collection. The fragments, archives, and particularly the houses form a treasure which is fundamental to the study of American domestic architecture from the late seventeenth century to the mid-Victorian period.

In 1910 the John Ward House (Fig. 1, Pl. I) stood at 37 St. Peter Street on land owned by Essex County. The county commissioners planned to build a new jail on the property and generously offered the building gratis to the Institute for safekeeping. George Francis Dow, secretary of the Institute, had the house moved a short distance to the grounds of the Institute, and then restored it extensively between 1910 and 1912. Dow, a man of prodigious energy and many talents, was then at the beginning of a long career in the mainstream of the budding historic-preservation movement. He had recently created three period rooms in the Institute museum—among the first of their kind in the country—and his pioneering restoration of the Ward house was based on his experience with these displays and on his familiarity with outdoor museums in Switzerland, Germany, and Scandinavia.

Pl. II. Hall of the John Ward House. This heavily framed room was mentioned in John Ward's will as the "best lower room." During the restoration, the original batten door leading to the lean-to was uncovered just to the left of a later, larger door. Dow furnished the room to its present appearance in an effort to present "a truthful picture of seventeenth century household life in Salem" (Essex Institute, *Annual Report,* 1909, p.18).

John Ward (c. 1653-1732), a currier by trade, probably began to build his house shortly after he purchased a lot on the east side of Prison Lane (now St. Peter Street) in 1684. Evidence in the framing and finish of the house indicates that it was built in three stages, the last of which preceded Ward's death in 1732. He first erected a heavily framed two-story structure with gables and an overhang, and an outside chimney on the eastern end. A slightly smaller and more lightly timbered two-story addition at the eastern end nearly doubled the size of the house. The lean-to, which is mentioned in Ward's will of 1732, was attached across the full length of the back of the house as the third stage of construction. The house was valued at £170 in 1732, and Ward's total estate amounted to more than £500. The inventory of his household goods includes beds and bedding, chairs, glassware, earthenware, silver, woolen apparel, linen, and quantities of "old" iron, pewter, brass, and wooden "household stuff."

The house remained in the Ward family until 1816, when it was sold at auction by Deborah Palfray, a granddaughter of John Ward. Temple Hardy of Salem purchased the "old mansion dwelling house" for $550, and opened a bakery in it which he operated for about forty years. After Hardy moved in 1855 the house was no longer occupied by its owner, and during the remaining years of the nineteenth century it served as a two-, three-, or four-unit apartment house. By 1910 it was seriously in need of repair.

Employing local contractors, Dow attempted to return the house to its appearance in 1732. He reconstructed the gables and fireplaces, and restored the central chimney; installed new casement windows everywhere except in the lean-to; and added a new front door and staircase based on examples from other seventeenth-century New England houses.

The two main downstairs rooms were outfitted with old and reproduction objects to represent a kitchen (Fig. 2) and a hall (Pl. II) of about 1700. Dow also installed three separate exhibits in the lean-to: what is known locally as a cent shop, complete with candies known as "Gibraltars," other penny candies, and additional small items; a weaving room with a mid-eighteenth-century loom; and an apothecary shop furnished with goods originally used in the nineteenth-century store of the Salem apothecary Dr. William Webb. The house was opened to the public in early 1912. It remains today an important example of early restoration philosophy and technique.

Despite the extensive changes made during the restoration, the Ward house still evokes in mass and outline a strong sense of the qualities of the first period of New England architecture. The peaked gables, the overhang, the asymmetrical plan, and the long sweep of the roof at the rear contribute to the angular and irregular form characteristic of this period. Inside, the exposed frame, with its chamfered posts and summer beams, the small original

Fig. 1. John Ward House at its original location, 37 St. Peter Street, in a photograph of 1889. Benjamin Ward inherited the house from his father in 1732 and it was probably he who modernized it by removing the massive gables and replacing the old-fashioned casements with the eighteenth-century sash windows visible here (see Pl. I). Early in the nineteenth century the chimney stack was modified when the house became a bakery, and a small section was added to the far, or eastern, end.

Fig. 2. George Francis Dow furnished the original downstairs eastern room of the Ward house as an early eighteenth-century kitchen. The featheredge sheathing is a reproduction, and the fireplace has been reconstructed. A small fireback with the convenient date 1684, obtained from another house, was installed in the fireplace in the 1920's.

Fig. 3. Western parlor of the Crowninshield-Bentley House (Pl. III). In the 1761 inventory of Captain John Crowninshield's estate this room was clearly furnished as a parlor with three tables, a clock, a large looking glass, a desk, nineteen chairs, and twenty-four framed pictures. The present woodwork probably dates from the 1790's, when the house was enlarged and remodeled. The room is now furnished as a parlor of the 1780's and early 1790's.

Pl. III. Crowninshield-Bentley House (built 1727-1729 with later eighteenth-century additions). The external symmetry of the formal façade belies the fact that the house grew in an organic manner dictated by the needs of its inhabitants.

Pl. IV. Eastern, or old, parlor of the Crowninshield-Bentley House. Furnished with objects made during the seventeenth and first half of the eighteenth century, this beautiful room suggests the way of life of the first occupants of the house. The set of leather-backed side chairs descended in the Curwen family of Salem, and the English caned-back chairs (of which one is visible here) are said to have been owned by the Clark family of Massachusetts. Under the looking glass (which is believed to have once hung in the John Hancock house in Boston) is a seventeenth-century oak chest with a Salem history.

back door, and the steeply rising staircase packed against the chimney are all reminders of the frankly functional aspects of the style.

In marked contrast is the Crowninshield-Bentley House (Pl. III) with its symmetrical façade, neoclassical doorway, and formally finished interior. The large central hallway and the well-executed woodwork throughout the house are elegant expressions of eighteenth-century Salem taste. Built for John Crowninshield (1696-1761), father and grandfather of several of Salem's most distinguished residents, the house was also the home of the famous minister and diarist William Bentley (1759-1819) from 1791 until his death (see Fig. 4). In 1959 the house was moved to the grounds of the Institute from its original location at 106 Essex Street and restored under the direction of Dean A. Fales Jr., then director of the Institute.

In typical New England fashion, this house grew with the families who occupied it. The original eastern rooms were built between 1727 and 1729, not long after John Crowninshield's marriage to Anstis Williams, when the couple still had only two children. With the arrival of their six other children it is little wonder that the house was extended to

Fig. 4. The Reverend William Bentley's room in the Crowninshield - Bentley House. Bentley boarded with Hannah Crowninshield and her daughter from 1791 until his death in 1819. During most of those years he lived in this room surrounded by the antiques and curiosities he avidly collected. Although few of his actual possessions now belong to the Essex Institute, the objects shown here are similar to those known to have belonged to him. These objects include a mezzotint of the Reverend Charles Brockwell, an early barometer, a Bible of 1791, a small fragment of Plymouth Rock, and numerous religious and scientific books. The simple windsor chairs and the Essex County curly-maple desk-and-bookcase perhaps resemble the furniture Bentley owned.

Fig. 5 Rear courtyard of the Peirce-Nichols House. These service buildings supported Jerathmiel Peirce's activities as one of the largest India traders in the country. The passage under the great keystone arch leads to gardens and to the North River, where his ships docked on their return from abroad.

Fig. 6. West parlor of the Peirce-Nichols House. This room retains the original bold Georgian woodwork installed at the time the house was built and attributed to Samuel McIntire (1757-1811). The 1827 inventory of Jerathmiel Peirce's estate indicates that this room was used as a dining room. Approximately eighty pieces of glassware and more than 250 pieces of ceramic wares were kept in this room, along with many tablecloths and napkins. Dinner was apparently served on two or three mahogany tables. The tiles surrounding the fireplace depict Aesop's fables (see pp. 1148-1155). According to tradition, they were taken as booty from a British vessel by John Leach, commander of the *Brutus* in 1780, and given by him to his brother-in-law Jerathmiel Peirce.

Fig. 7. Front elevation for the Assembly House (Pl. VI), by McIntire, c. 1796. This drawing, although neither signed nor dated, bears measurements in McIntire's handwriting and is on paper which McIntire used between 1795 and 1804, according to Fiske Kimball. In many respects this elevation is a linear and abstract interpretation of the designs of Charles Bulfinch and, ultimately, Robert Adam. Also preserved in the Institute's archives is a working sketch by Daniel Bancroft, McIntire's chief builder, based on this elevation. *Essex Institute archives; photograph by courtesy of the Essex Institute.*

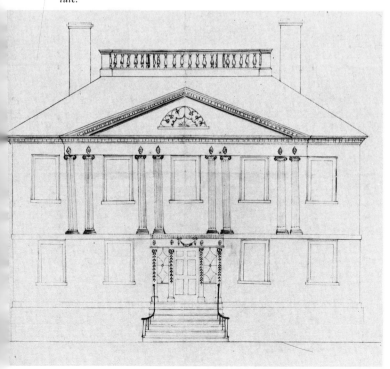

the west of the entrance hall sometime before 1761. After Crowninshield's death in that year his descendants owned the house in common and continued to occupy it until well into the nineteenth century. In 1794 Bentley recorded in his diary that extensive alterations and improvements were being made to the house.[2] A second kitchen and a room were added to the rear of the western half of the house, forming what is known as a Beverly jog. The woodwork in the western parlor probably also dates from this time (Fig. 3).

At the time of the restoration in 1959 and 1960 Abbott L. Cummings recorded much of what workmen found when they peeled away layers of later paint and paneling. The eastern, or old, parlor (Pl. IV) had been considerably modernized but marks around the fireplace indicated the width of the original bolection molding. This and applied moldings similar to those found in the upper rooms were restored to the fireplace wall. The dado and window trim dating to the late eighteenth century were left intact. Scraping revealed that the original color of the woodwork was an Indian red and that the door to the hall had been grained around 1800.

Directly above the eastern parlor is the room Bentley occupied (Fig. 4). It has been furnished as it might have been in his time. The original bolection molding and a later heavy mantel were found intact on the fireplace wall, and investigation revealed that these had been painted green in contrast to the blue found on the rest of the wall.

The woodwork in the western parlor (Fig. 3) probably dates from the late eighteenth-century renovation carried out by Captain Benjamin Crowninshield, a grandson of John Crowninshield. The fine featheredge paneling, eared overmantel panels, denticulated cornice, and sliding interior shutters are appropriate for what was considered to be the "best parlor" as early as 1761.

Other interesting features of the interior are the bolection molding and raised paneling in the west front room and the

delicate miniature chimney breast in the garret. The furnishings in both rooms resemble as closely as possible those given in the 1761 inventory of John Crowninshield's estate. In the old, or eastern, kitchen the restorers discovered the original cast-iron fireback still in the huge fireplace. In this and the western kitchen an extensive collection of eighteenth-century kitchen equipment is on display.

In much the same way that Charles Bulfinch transformed the look of Boston, Samuel McIntire changed the architectural character of Salem between about 1780 and his death in 1811.[3] The Institute has been fortunate to obtain houses which illustrate each phase of his career. The Peirce-Nichols House at 80 Federal Street (cover), probably built in 1782, was McIntire's first major work, and is unique in that parts of the house were remodeled under his direction in 1801. It combines under one roof superb examples of McIntire's Georgian and Adamesque periods and demonstrates the great changes in style which took place over twenty years.

Bold pilasters at the corners and a pedimented porch in the Doric order provide the major ornamentation on the front façade; the window caps act as a broken stringcourse to divide horizontally the otherwise unadorned clapboard exterior. A balustrade surrounds the hipped roof. Of particular interest are the surviving stable, countinghouse, and other structures facing the rear courtyard (Fig. 5). Designing such an estate was a formidable accomplishment for McIntire, then only in his mid-twenties.

Jerathmiel Peirce (1747-1827), the original owner of the house, could gaze out of his third-story window over the top of the outbuildings and see his ships sail up the North River and dock virtually in his back yard. Peirce was trained as a leather dresser but after seeing service in the Revolution he embarked on a career as a merchant which brought him great wealth as well as many tribulations. He finally went bankrupt in 1826 and was forced to sell the house at public auction. It was purchased by George and Martha Johonnot, wealthy friends of the family, who deeded it back to Jerathmiel's son-in-law George Nichols in 1840. The house was legally transferred to the Institute in 1917 by Martha, Charlotte, and Augusta Nichols, great-granddaughters of Jerathmiel. The last of these three unmarried sisters died in 1935, at which time the Institute assumed full control of the house.[4]

The young McIntire's conservative source of inspiration for many details of the mantel and overmantel in the west parlor (Fig. 6) and for the Doric order on the exterior was Batty Langley's outdated volume of designs entitled *City and Country Builder's and Workman's Treasury of Designs,* first published in London in 1740. This bold Georgian woodwork contrasts sharply with the delicate Adamesque carving and plaster composition ornament found in the hall, east parlor (Pl. V), and upstairs bedroom. These rooms were refurbished in 1801 for the wedding of Sally Peirce and

Pl. VI. Assembly House, 138 Federal Street (built 1782, remodeled 1796-1798). Samuel McIntire was engaged to remodel the Assembly House, turning it from a public meeting hall into an elaborate and fashionable dwelling.

Pl. VII. East front parlor of the Assembly House. This room is now furnished with China Trade furniture of the mid- to late nineteenth century. Such parlor sets of Oriental furniture were popular in the Victorian era and reflect the cosmopolitan nature of Salem taste during these years. The intricately carved furniture, reminiscent of the rococo revival, makes a sharp contrast with the more austere McIntire woodwork.

Fig. 8. Front doorway and portico of the Assembly House. The delicate swag, ribbon, and bellflower motifs of McIntire's doorway are shadowed by the portico that was added to the house about 1840. The Ionic columns were carved to match McIntire's delicate pilasters. The eclectic nature of the cornice ornament and the bold relief carving of the grapevine in the frieze are characteristic of the mid-nineteenth century and resemble designs found in the pattern books of Minard Lafever.

George Nichols, and it is likely that the wooden front fence with its classical urns (restored in the 1920's) was also added at this time.

The generosity of members of the family and friends has enabled the Institute to reinstall in the Peirce-Nichols House many of the original furnishings, some of which are listed in an extensive household inventory taken in 1829. For example, a set of six small settees attributed to McIntire and listed in the inventory as "4 Window Settees and 2 Recess. Do., patch cover'd" are still in their original positions in the east parlor (see Pl. V). Other family furnishings in this room include a pier glass, the overmantel looking glass, and several chairs.

In 1782 a group of about thirty prominent Salem men, including William Stearns, Jonathan Waldo, Edward Augustus Holyoke, Elias Hasket Derby, and Samuel Blyth, combined their resources to erect a new assembly house, where balls, dances, concerts, lectures, theatricals, and other social and cultural events could be held. Such gathering places were common features in eighteenth-century England—the rooms at Bath being a famous example—and could be found in Portsmouth, New Hampshire; Alexandria, Virginia; Philadelphia, and other American towns.

Salem at that time was without an appropriate setting for its public entertainments. An early assembly hall, built in 1766 near the corner of Cambridge and Chestnut streets, had been converted into a meetinghouse in 1774. Washington Hall, Concert Hall, and Hamilton Hall, future locations for these affairs, were not built until after 1792.

The exact appearance of the Assembly House erected in 1782 by the proprietors will probably never be known, nor has the name of its architect or builder come down to us. We do know that it had a ballroom perhaps two stories high, with a musician's gallery, "elegant" paintings, and a glass chandelier from Boston. Drawing rooms were furnished with chairs, sofas, and tables for gaming. Visits by Lafayette in 1784 and President Washington in 1789 were merely the highlights in a busy schedule of music, dancing, theater, and even exhibitions of waxworks.

With the completion in 1792 of Washington Hall, a new assembly room in a building called the Stearns Block, the center of festivities in Salem gradually shifted away from the Assembly House. In 1796 Jonathan Waldo (1754-1815), one of the original proprietors, acquired full possession of the house, and in 1798 he sold it to Samuel Putnam (1768-1853), a famous Salem lawyer.

Either Waldo or Putnam engaged McIntire to turn the Assembly House into a fashionable dwelling (Pl. VI), and

Fig. 9. Stairway of the Assembly House. Fiske Kimball attributed this stairway to McIntire, calling it the "earliest of the surviving examples" in McIntire's Adamesque style (*Mr. Samuel McIntire, Carver: The Architect of Salem,* Portland, Maine, 1940, p. 39). However, it is possible that the simple stair dates to the original building of 1782. The doorway on the landing may originally have led to a ballroom or possibly to a musician's gallery. Some question exists as to whether the pilasters and portrait bust (attributed to the Skillin family of Boston) date to the original building or to McIntire's remodeling.

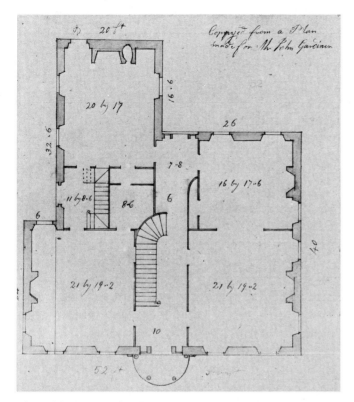

Fig. 10. Floor plan of the Gardner-Pingree House (Pl. VIII), by McIntire. This plan from McIntire's scrapbook of designs bears his handwriting. It closely corresponds to the Gardner-Pingree House as built. Spatial innovations characteristic of the neoclassical period include the double parlor (Pl. IX) and the butler's pantry inserted between the dining room and the kitchen in the ell. *Essex Institute archives; Essex Institute photograph.*

his work is documented by a front elevation (Fig. 7) preserved among his papers at the Institute. McIntire enriched the house by adding four pairs of Ionic pilasters to the second story of a flat-boarded façade, and a broad pediment incorporating a semicircular fanlight across the front of the hipped roof. The central doorway was elaborated with rosettes and bellflowers, which have been somewhat obscured since the present porch was added about 1840 (Fig. 8). Measured and elegant, the entire façade is in keeping with McIntire's adoption of the neoclassical style in 1793. Daniel Bancroft, McIntire's chief builder, handled the basic carpentry.

The decoration of the east front parlor (Pl. VII) dates to McIntire's remodeling. The carved denticulated cornice and composition ornaments of the mantel are typical of McIntire's work and are probably derived from the pattern books of William and James Pain. In harmony with the exterior design, McIntire framed the recesses on either side of the chimney with fluted Ionic pilasters. Similar pilasters and capitals with cherub's heads in the hallway also appear to have been designed by McIntire. The central stairway leads to a landing where a grandiose pedimented doorway flanked by pilasters leads to the rear of the house (Fig. 9).

The Assembly House was given to the Institute by Mary Silver Smith in 1965, and was opened to the public in 1972. The house is furnished to represent the different generations of Salem families who lived there from the last years of the eighteenth through the nineteenth century. The east front parlor contains many elaborately carved pieces of mid- to late nineteenth-century furniture from Zanzibar, China, and India. The west front room on the ground floor is furnished as a dining room, with Chippendale and early

classical revival pieces. On the second floor, the east front room is arranged as a bedroom, dominated by a massive colonial revival bed and highlighted by two examples of the work of the Salem cabinetmaker William Hook (1777-1867). Across the hall, the west front room has been furnished as a Victorian sitting room of about 1870, and includes a magnificent set of rococo revival furniture with a Northampton, Massachusetts, history. In short, under the guidance of David B. Little, director, and Huldah Payson, curator, the Institute staff has restored the house in such a way that its rich and varied history is acknowledged and preserved.

The Gardner-Pingree House (Pl. VIII) is the masterpiece of McIntire's mature style. It was built in 1804 and 1805 for John Gardner (1771-1847), the eldest son of John and Sarah Derby Gardner and a grandson of the famous Salem merchant Richard Derby. By 1804 Gardner was a prosperous importer and he sought to display his new wealth by erecting this magnificent dwelling on Essex Street just off Washington Square. McIntire was the logical choice to design such a showpiece, and his connection with the house is documented by a floor plan in his hand (Fig. 10) in which the traditional four-square plan has been altered by Federal innovations.

Elegance and restraint characterize this jewel of a house. The surface of the beautiful brick façade is ornamented only by stone lintels set flush with the outside wall and two

Fig. 11. Detail of the mantel in the front parlor of the Gardner-Pingree House. This and a nearly identical mantel in the rear parlor contain many motifs characteristic of McIntire's work, including fruit and flowers and sheaves of wheat. The columns may be based on a design for "¼ columns, with antique caps, and sprigs of bay twisting round the columns" illustrated in Pl. 16 of William and James Pain, *Pain's British Palladio* (London, 1793), a copy of which was probably in McIntire's library.

Pl. VIII. Gardner-Pingree House (built 1804-1805), 128 Essex Street. The masterpiece of Samuel McIntire's fully developed Adamesque style, the house is today the only intact survivor of a number of neoclassical mansions that once lined both sides of this part of Essex Street.

Pl. IX. Double parlor of the Gardner-Pingree House. McIntire's interiors rely on the repetition and integration of ornamental motifs for their visual impact. In this room the ornaments on the mantels reappear in the cornice, chair rail, and doorframes. The Aubusson rugs, China Trade garniture, and graceful neoclassical furniture successfully convey the surroundings of Salem's early nineteenth-century merchants. The wallpaper panel over the mantel is from the series Les Douze Mois, designed by Fragonard Fils in 1808 and printed by Joseph Dufour in Paris. It and six others panels from the series were installed in the house during and after restoration.

stringcourses, painted white, which divide the façade into three sections. The portico has been carefully but subtly integrated into the design since its cornice line forms part of the lower stringcourse. Typical of McIntire's work at this period, the portico has both Corinthian columns and Corinthian pilasters which exhibit the finely carved detail echoed in the interior.

Fiske Kimball felt that the lavish interiors of the Gardner-Pingree House rivaled those of the famous Elias Hasket Derby mansion. Their harmonious proportions, rhythmic interrelationships, and carved and applied composition ornament reveal what William H. Pierson Jr. described as McIntire's "exquisite sense of beauty and ... deep poetic feeling for the qualities of wood."[5] In the double parlor (Pl. IX) the mantelpieces (see Fig. 11) are the focus of attention. The dish of fruit in the center is flanked by swags and rosettes; the projecting blocks of the entablature bear sheaves of wheat, and the whole is capped with a molded cornice containing a row of dentils. Similar features are repeated above the wide doorway that separates the parlors and above the doors leading to the hall.

Fig. 12. Crowninshield Memorial Room in the Gardner-Pingree House. Furnished in the neoclassical style, this room also contains many small imported objects which reflect the international tastes of Salem merchants in the early nineteenth century. As this is the only room in the house which lacks a closet, it may originally have been used as a drawing room. Although this and the other woodwork in the house has been painted white, the ground of the panels in the mantelpiece may originally have been colored light pink, green, or blue, with the low-relief decoration picked out in white, in accordance with the prevailing taste.

This wide and inviting hall also received McIntire's close attention. It is divided in half by an archway that is decorated with combinations of reeding, fluting, moldings, and plaster rosettes. The wooden cornice has small curved brackets similar to those found in Plate 18 of Asher Benjamin's *Country Builder's Assistant,* which was first published in 1797. The pierced balusters of the stairway repeat a pattern found in the chair rail in the double parlor.

The most elaborate upstairs room is the southeast room on the second floor (Fig. 12) which was furnished as a memorial to the Crowninshield family by Louise du Pont Crowninshield, who did so much to assist in the restoration of this and the Institute's other houses. The center of the mantel here is embellished with a composition ornament depicting a reclining figure of Plenty, her cornucopia, and an attendant cherub. At the sides of the mantel are sheaves of wheat.

The heirs of David Pingree (1841-1932) gave the house to the Institute in 1933 to insure its preservation, and thus brought to an end nearly a century of ownership by the Pingree family. During that period many changes had been made to modernize the appearance and convenience of the house, including the installation of Victorian marble mantelpieces and coal-burning-fireplace grates. Fortunately, most of the original mantels had been carefully stored in the attic, and the restorers had only to reinstall them in the

proper rooms. The dining-room mantel was apparently lost and a later McIntire mantel from the Pickman house on Essex Street was substituted for it. The stair balusters were reproduced from an original which was found in the Institute's collections during the process of restoration.

Among the most interesting features of the Gardner-Pingree House as it stands today are the fine wallpapers which were installed throughout the house during restoration. The back parlor was papered with six panels of the series Les Douze Mois, designed by Fragonard Fils in 1808 and printed by Joseph Dufour of Paris, and a reproduction of an original border paper which was found on the east wall of the room. The southeast room on the third floor is covered with two early nineteenth-century French grisaille papers entitled Venetian Scenes and Banks of the Rhine which were found in houses in Essex County. Perhaps the most unusual paper, however, is that installed in the third-floor hall. Painted by Michele Felice Cornè (1752-1845), this paper was originally in the Timothy Lindall house in Salem.

The Gardner-Pingree House is furnished to reflect the cosmopolitan nature of Salem life during its heyday as a thriving center of international trade. While most of the outstanding furniture was made locally in Essex County or Boston, several fine examples of Chinese furniture in the Western taste and many smaller decorative objects—silver, ceramics, glass, and paintings, among others—are reminders of Salem's extensive interests in the Orient, the West Indies, England, and Europe.

The Andrew-Safford House is perhaps the most imposing and monumental of the many three-story brick mansions erected in Salem during the Federal period (Pl. X, Fig. 13). It is the masterpiece of an as-yet unknown architect or housewright, but in a general sense it owes much to Salem's tradition of neoclassical architecture as established by McIntire and developed after his death by such men as Jabez Smith and David Lord. Many of the decorative details are taken, sometimes exactly but more often loosely, from the pattern books and builders' guides published by Asher Benjamin (1773-1845).

Facing east on what was once Newbury Street and is now Washington Square West, the house is massive and very vertical in feeling. The smooth brick façade rises from the stone foundation to the balustrade without the interruption of rustication, quoins, stringcourses, or other decorative details. The evenly spaced windows set flush to the wall force the eye to concentrate on the elaborate Corinthian entrance portico and the Palladian window above it. The most dramatic feature is the row of four massive Doric columns along the south side facing the garden (Fig. 13). The Reverend William Bentley, who looked on as the last of these imposing pine shafts was raised on October 23, 1819, recognized that they represented "building in true as well as great style."[6]

Periodic entries in the diary of the ever-watchful Bentley tell us that the house was built over a span of about eighteen months during 1818 and 1819. The first owner was John Andrew (1774-1829), who paid for the house with his earnings as a commission merchant in the Russia trade and probably with part of a considerable inheritance received by his wife, Catharine, from her father, the wealthy John Forrester. The Andrew family lived in the house until 1860. After a brief period of ownership by the Smith and Creamer families, James Osborne Safford (1819-1883) purchased the house in 1871, and members of his family lived there until it became part of the Essex Institute in 1947. Since 1955 the house has been the residence of the Institute's director.

Several rooms on the first floor are now open to the public for the first time on a regular basis. The front parlor (Pl. XI), or drawing room as it is called in John Andrew's inventory, is perhaps the most elaborate room in the house. It is embellished with a fine Italian marble mantelpiece and carving by Joseph True (1785-1873), who billed Andrew for carving fifty ornaments. A surviving panel of wallpaper, one of the scenes from the series entitled *Les Amours de Psyché* printed by Dufour of Paris in 1816, is a reminder of the many elegant French papers originally used throughout the house, and an indication of Andrew's fine taste and high ambitions.

Across the wide hallway is what is now known as the Victorian parlor (Pl. XII). The rich woodwork probably dates to a remodeling by the Saffords in the 1870's.

The importance of this house is enhanced by the survival of its original barn, formal gardens, summerhouse, and the brick walls, iron gateways, and fences that enclose the property. The whole ensemble forms a delightful estate of the early nineteenth century.

The Institute's superb houses are only part of Salem's rich architectural legacy. Houses of the seventeenth, eighteenth, and nineteenth centuries can still be found on Essex, Federal, Broad, Chestnut, Derby, Turner, and other streets. Many of these buildings are still privately owned and their quality has long been recognized. As early as 1686, John Dunton found "many fine Houses" in Salem,[7] and John Adams commented in 1766 that Salem's "houses are the most elegant and grand that I have seen in any of the maritime towns."[8] The duc de La Rochefoucault-Liancourt simply said in 1796 that Salem was "one of the handsomest small towns in the United States."[9] Due to the efforts of the Essex Institute, several public institutions, and many individuals, this is still true today.

Fig. 13. South façade of the Andrew-Safford House (Pl. X). On October 21, 1819, the Reverend William Bentley noted in his diary that "this week Capt. John Andrew is raising his four large columns on the south side of his house. These are the largest ever raised in Salem. They stand on the basement story on the S.W. part of the house. The base is of free stone, the shafts fluted, of pine" (*The Diary of William Bentley, D.D.,* Salem, 1914; reprinted Gloucester, 1962, vol. 4, p. 623).

[1] This essay is based primarily on a series of articles which originally appeared in the *Essex Institute Historical Collections:* Abbott Lowell Cummings, "The House and Its People," vol. 97, no. 2 (April 1961), pp. 82-97; Dean A. Fales Jr., "The Furnishings of the House," vol. 97, no. 2, pp. 98-128; Barbara M. and Gerald W. R. Ward, "The John Ward House: A Social and Architectural History," vol. 110, no. 1 (January 1974), pp. 3-32; Gerald W. R. Ward, "Additional Notes on the Crowninshield-Bentley House," vol. 111, no. 1 (January 1975), pp. 1-11; "The Gardner-Pingree House," vol. 111, no. 2 (April 1975), pp. 81-98; "The Peirce-Nichols House," vol. 111, no. 3 (July 1975), pp. 161-195; "The Assembly House," vol. 111, no. 4 (October 1975), pp. 241-266; and "The Andrew-Safford House," vol. 112, no. 2 (April 1976), pp. 59-88. Unless otherwise noted, documentation and additional references for the statements made here can be found in these articles, which were reissued by the Essex Institute in 1976 in a series of booklets.

[2] *The Diary of William Bentley, D. D.* (Salem, 1914; reprinted Gloucester, 1962), vol. 3, p. 463.

[3] The definitive discussion of McIntire's career is Fiske Kimball, *Mr. Samuel McIntire, Carver: The Architect of Salem* (Portland, Maine, 1940). We have relied extensively on this book for those sections of this article that deal with McIntire houses.

[4] Entertaining biographical sketches of Jerathmiel Peirce and his descendants may be found in Susan Nichols Pulsifer, *Witch's Breed: The Peirce-Nichols Family of Salem* (Cambridge, 1967).

Pl. X. Andrew-Safford House, 13 Washington Square West (built 1818-1819). The house was one of several mansions built in 1818 and 1819 around Washington Square. The Reverend William Bentley noted in 1819 that "great labour has been bestowed on Washington Square," and that "the many new buildings have justified this care of this section of the town" (*Diary of William Bentley,* vol. 4, p. 605). In 1919 the Salem architectural historian Phil M. Riley stated that the Andrew-Safford estate, "embracing a stable at the right in harmony with the house and a fine old formal garden at the left, exemplifies as do few others the best that money could provide in Salem a century ago" (Frank Cousins and Phil M. Riley, *The Colonial Architecture of Salem,* Boston, 1919, p. 95).

[5] William H. Pierson Jr., *American Buildings and Their Architects: The Colonial and Neoclassical Styles* (Garden City, New York, 1970), p. 222.

[6] *Diary of William Bentley,* vol. 4, p. 624.

[7] Quoted in George Francis Dow, ed., *Two Centuries of Travel in Essex County* (Topsfield, Massachusetts, 1921), p. 34.

[8] *Ibid.,* p. 87.

[9] *Ibid.,* p. 178.

Pl. XI. Front parlor of the Andrew-Safford House. The elaborate Empire parlor set was a wedding present to Catharine Peabody Gardner from her father, Joseph Peabody, in 1827. Purchased in Italy by Peabody's agent, the set consists of six side chairs, two so-called Récamier couches, one large sofa, and two small sofas. The set was refurbished in 1974 with the aid of a grant from the Massachusetts Council on the Arts and Humanities.

Pl. XII. Victorian parlor in the Andrew-Safford House. The Renaissance revival table in the center of the room is a recent addition to the Institute's collection (see ANTIQUES, May 1977, p. 973, Pl. XVII, Fig. 23, where it was illustrated in its original setting in the Samuel Bubier house in Lynn). The richly carved woodwork was probably installed by the Safford family in the 1870's. The painted canvas floorcloth dates from the middle of the nineteenth century.

Living with antiques

The Lindens, Washington, D.C.

BY NANCY A. ILIFF

Fig. 1. The Lindens was built in 1754 for Robert "King" Hooper (1709–1790) in Danvers, Massachusetts. The design has been attributed to Peter Harrison (1716–1775) by John Fitzhugh Millar *(The Architects of the American Colonies* [Barre, Massachusetts, 1968], p. 158). The south façade of this wooden house simulates ashlar masonry and is one of only a few examples in America of painted and sanded rustication. Others are Mount Vernon and the Redwood Library in Newport, Rhode Island, which was designed by Harrison. The Lindens now stands at 2401 Kalorama Road, N.W., Washington, D.C., to which site it was moved in the 1930's by its present owner, Mrs. George Maurice Morris, and her late husband. It is on the National Register of Historic Places. Another view of the house appears on the cover. *Photographs are by Helga Photo Studio.*

VERY EARLY in her marriage to the late George Maurice Morris, Miriam Hubbard Morris began to collect antiques. The search for a suitable dwelling in which to house them took Mrs. Morris from Charleston, South Carolina, to Maine. When she found the Lindens, in Danvers, Massachusetts, it had been bought by Israel Sack, who planned to sell its components piecemeal. Indeed, the drawing-room woodwork had already gone to a museum.

Fig. 2. The central entrance hall is twelve feet wide and forty-two feet long. On its walls are panels from the three complete sets of block-printed nineteenth-century French wallpapers in the house. At the left is *Les Incas,* first printed by Dufour et Leroy in 1826 and inspired by Jean François Marmontel's novel *Les Incas, ou la Destruction de l'Empire de Perou* of 1777 (see Pl. I). At the right is *Télemaque dans l'Ile de Calypso,* printed by Dufour et Leroy in 1825 (see also Pl. II). The wallpapers were probably hung in the middle of the nineteenth century by the Peabodys, who then owned the Lindens and who acquired the papers from a factory in Alsace.

Fig. 3. In the second-floor stair hall is displayed the third of the three block-printed French wallpapers in the house, the *Voyage d'Antênor,* printed by Joseph Dufour et Cie c. 1814 (see also Pl. III). The window curtains are of eighteenth-century raw silk. To the right of the window is a Philadelphia mahogany tall-case clock, 1750–1770, with *William Huston* engraved on the silver face. The walnut Pennsylvania drop-leaf table, 1720–1750, is flanked by a pair of Newport side chairs attributed to the Townsend-Goddard workshop, 1740–1760. The hanging lantern was made in England c. 1780.

Pl. I. On this wall of the central hall Francisco Pizarro is depicted landing in Peru in a panel from *Les Incas* (see Fig. 2). The marble-topped mahogany table was made in New York State c. 1765. The walnut Chippendale chairs are from a set of six made in Philadelphia c. 1765 for the Billmyer family (see also Fig. 4). The bill of sale for the chairs is in the Germantown Historical Society. The mirror wall sconces are English, 1740–1760.

The Morrises bought the house and decided to move it to Washington, D.C. Under the direction of Walter Macomber, once the resident architect at Colonial Williamsburg, the house was dismantled over a period of seven weeks, loaded onto six freight cars, and shipped to Washington. Ground was broken in 1934 at 2401 Kalorama Road, N.W., the present address of the Lindens. Since the housewarming in November 1937, more than eighty thousand visitors have been through the Lindens, for as Mrs. Morris once said, "After my family, the most absorbing interest in my life has been the Lindens. My heartfelt wish is that it may bring continued interest and enjoyment to many generations yet to come." She has often remarked of the house, "The only possible way in the world I think I deserve it is to share it."

Pl. II. On this wall of the central hall is a scene from *Télemaque dans l'Ile de Calypso* (see Fig. 2). The oval walnut Chippendale drop-leaf table is flanked by two Philadelphia chairs of 1760–1780. The elaborate and inventive balusters are reminiscent of those on the great stair in the Jeremiah Lee mansion in Marblehead, Massachusetts (see ANTIQUES for December 1977, p. 1165, Fig. 1, and p. 1166, Fig. 2).

Pl. III. This corner of the second-floor stair hall is occupied by a mahogany table made in Salem c. 1785 which has a top of unusual shape. The walnut chairs flanking it were made in New York State, 1750–1780. On the wall is a scene from the *Voyage d'Anténor* (see also Fig. 3). The stenciled border on the floor is one of several in the Lindens that were executed c. 1790.

Pl. IV. The paneling in the drawing room is a replica of the original, which was sold to the William Rockhill Nelson Gallery and Atkins Museum of Fine Arts in Kansas City, Missouri, before the Morrises bought the Lindens. In front of the splendid mahogany Philadelphia sofa of 1750–1780 is a mahogany tea table made in Newport and attributed to the Townsend-Goddard workshop, 1740–1760. Above the New Jersey mahogany dressing table of 1720–1750 hangs a fine New England looking glass, 1760–1770. The chandelier is English, c. 1760. The rug is a Sultanabad. The valance over the damask curtains is copied from an eighteenth-century English one in the Philadelphia Museum of Art.

Pl. V. The cherry desk-and-bookcase at this end of the drawing room is probably of Maryland origin, 1750–1760. Drawn up to it is a walnut roundabout chair made in Philadelphia, 1750–1780. The easy chair and mahogany tilt-top table were also made in Philadelphia, 1750–1780.

Fig. 4. The cupboard in this corner of the drawing room (see also Pls. IV and V) retains the original black and white marbleizing. On the shelves are pieces of mid-eighteenth-century China Trade porcelain bearing the arms of the Ross family of Balnagown Castle in Scotland, from which Mrs. Morris' mother came. Mrs. Morris found and acquired the porcelain in London. The mahogany Marlborough-leg easy chair was made in Philadelphia, 1750–1780. The eighteenth-century mahogany card table, also from Philadelphia, is one of a pair in the room. It is flanked by two of a set of six walnut side chairs made in Philadelphia c. 1765 for the Billmyer family (see also Pl. I). The Waterford or English glass candle bracket, c. 1760, is also one of a pair in the room. The bell cord is a duplicate of one in the Victoria and Albert Museum in London that originally hung in Ham House in Surrey.

Fig. 5. The library has been restored to its original Spanish-brown color. Above the New England walnut desk of 1750–1780 hangs an English reverse painting on glass with mirrors below it, 1730–1740. The curtains are of English block-printed linen of c. 1820. The eighteenth-century fire bucket to the left of the desk bears the English royal coat of arms. Most of the lighting in the house is by electrified candles, each containing a seven-watt bulb. Henry Francis du Pont allowed Mrs. Morris to use candles of this design, which were invented for the Winterthur Museum.

Fig. 6. After the house was moved, Mrs. Morris created this basement room to resemble an old tavern dance hall. The brick and beams are original to the house; the floor boards and pine sheathing are from eighteenth-century houses that have been demolished. What appears to be the ceiling in the foreground is a hinged panel that can be lowered to divide the room into two. The American trestle table of maple with a pine top, 1680–1700, still bears its original Spanish-brown paint. The walnut dresser at the end of the room was made in Wales, 1740–1780.

Fig. 7. The mahogany bed in the pink room was made in Salem, 1750–1780. The eighteenth-century *toile de Jouy* hangings and curtains are stamped *manufacture de S. D. M. Oberkampf.* The mahogany serpentine-front chest of drawers was made in New England, 1760–1780. Above it hangs an American Chippendale looking glass. The looking glass to the right of the bed is labeled "Bittle & Cooper,/Burnish Gilders, No. 3, Schollay's Buildings . . ./Keep Constantly on Hand a General Assortment of/Looking Glasses—The Newest Fashions./Warranted faithfully made, and at as low prices as can be pur-/chased at any other Store in Boston. . . ." As there are eighteenth-century precedents for them, Venetian blinds are used throughout the house.

Pl. VI. The mahogany three-section tripod table in the dining room is English of the late eighteenth century. Drawn up to it are some of a set of twelve New York State mahogany chairs, c. 1775, which once belonged to the Revolutionary War general Matthew Clarkson. The design of the back of these chairs was adapted from Chippendale's *Gentleman and Cabinet-Maker's Director* (3rd ed., London, 1762), No. 12. Nine chairs with an identical back but with straight legs are known: six in the Governor's Palace in Colonial Williamsburg, two in the American Wing of the Metropolitan Museum of Art, and one in the Henry Ford Museum in Dearborn, Michigan. The silver epergne, made in London c. 1765, is marked by Emick Romer. Above the English mahogany serving table of c. 1740 hangs an eighteenth-century mahogany and gilt Philadelphia looking glass.

Pl. VII. This is the largest of the bedrooms. On the floor are stenciled a complete ellipse and half an ellipse. It has been suggested that the latter may have been intended to ward off witches. All the original doors in the house have HH (heaven and hell) or HL (Holy Lord) hinges and are designed so that the paneling forms a double cross. It was believed that witches could not come through a double-crossed door. The mahogany New England slant-front desk of 1760–1780 has a serpentine front and, a rarity, gadrooning on the feet and skirt. The desk was the frontispiece in Antiques for November 1944. The gilded looking glass above it was probably made in Philadelphia, 1760–1780. The Philadelphia tripod table and chairs of 1750–1780 are mahogany.

Pl. VIII. Along this wall of the bedroom shown in Pl. VII is a very fine Philadelphia mahogany chest on chest, 1750–1780. It is pictured and discussed as one of the best of its kind in Albert Sack's *Fine Points of Furniture: Early American* (New York, 1950), p. 118. The easy chair with hairy-paw feet, 1750–1780, was originally thought to be English (see Antiques for January 1936, p. 18, and February 1938, p. 78), but wood analysis revealed American, specifically Southern, secondary woods.

Pl. IX. The blue bedroom is Mrs.
Morris' own. The bed and window
hangings are crewelwork of Charles
II's time, which also covers the shades
of two discreet reading lamps
mounted at the top of the headposts
of the bed. The Cromwellian chair, c.
1660, still has its original turkeywork
upholstery. The New England high
chest of 1720–1730 is veneered with
burl walnut.

Pl. X. This view of the blue bedroom shows a burl-walnut-veneered William and Mary high chest with trumpet legs that was made in New England, 1700–1710. It is illustrated as one of the best of its kind in Sack's *Fine Points of Furniture* (p. 173). On the wall are framed pieces of Charles II needlework. The New England maple banister-back chair of 1700–1710 bears its original black paint. The fireplace in each bedroom is flanked by closets, one for clothes, the other for powdering wigs. The latter closet in each case has been made into a bathroom.

Pl. XI. In this corner of the blue bedroom is a walnut New England bunfooted chest of drawers of c. 1700, over which hangs a seventeenth-century English looking glass which is said to have come from Blenheim Palace in Oxfordshire, England. A seventeenth-century English beadwork box stands on the chest of drawers. The American beech chairs were made c. 1690. The rug is a Feraghan.

The first Harrison Gray Otis House

BY RICHARD NYLANDER, *Curator of collections, Society for the Preservation of New England Antiquities*

THE HARRISON GRAY OTIS House on Cambridge Street in Boston (Fig. 1) is today the city's only freestanding late eighteenth-century town house, although when it was built it was one of many impressive residences in Boston. As recently restored, the house is important for what it tells us about taste and decoration in the early years of the republic.

The three-story brick structure is associated with two men who, working together, left an indelible stamp on the architectural character and topography of Boston. They are Charles Bulfinch, the architect, and his client, Harrison Gray Otis, a promising young lawyer with an active interest in real estate.[1]

When Henry Wansey visited Boston in 1794, he described the buildings as "indifferent," and said that they reminded him of "the old-fashioned towns of England." He noted, however, that "the part of town called New or West Boston, is an exception to this, for the houses there are all neat and elegant (of brick) with handsome entrances and door cases and a flight of steps up to the entrance."[2]

Wansey's general impression was probably an apt description of Bowdoin Square, the fashionable residential area in the mid-eighteenth century where Bulfinch and Otis had both grown up. Indeed, among the "neat and elegant" buildings were undoubtedly the early efforts which Bulfinch had designed for his friends shortly after his return to his

Pl. I. Dining room (see also Fig. 5). The portrait of Harrison Gray Otis (1765-1848) is by Gilbert Stuart (1755-1828), 1809. The table descended in the Appleton family (see ANTIQUES for May 1975, p. 881, Pl. III; pp. 886-887); the twelve chairs belonged to Mary Otis, half sister of Harrison Gray Otis. "It has not fallen to my lot to meet a man more skilled in the useful art of entertaining his friends than Otis," wrote John Quincy Adams to his father in 1816 (quoted in Samuel Eliot Morison, *Harrison Gray Otis, 1765-1848: The Urbane Federalist*, Boston, 1969, p. 193).

Fig. 1. The first Harrison Gray Otis House, built in 1795 at 141 Cambridge Street, Boston. *Except as noted, photographs are by Richard Cheek.*

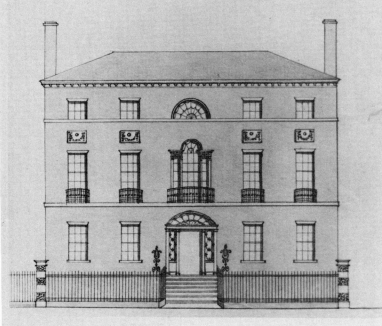

Fig. 2. Elevation for the first Harrison Gray Otis House by Charles Bulfinch (1763-1844). The inscription, in Mrs. Otis's hand, reads: "Designed by C. Bulfinch about 1796 for Copley land and excepting the second story windows, precisely the front of what Mr. H. G. Otis called The Brick House in Lynde & Chambers Street" (see n. 6). *Massachusetts Historical Society; photograph by George M. Cushing.*

native town in 1787 from a tour of Europe which had begun in 1785. In style these buildings were totally different from anything previously built in Boston, for they expressed the ideals of the wealthy aristocracy that had sprung up after the Revolution.

Otis began building what he called "The Brick House" (see Fig. 2) in 1795 on land given to him by his father-in-law. Cambridge Street, leading west from Bowdoin Square, was a natural choice of location since it was close to Otis's family and friends. The severity of the façade Bulfinch created in his elevation (Fig. 2) makes it atypical of his previous work. It lacks the engaged pilasters and recessed arches of the Tontine Crescent (1793-1794) and the Joseph Coolidge Jr. House (1795), although he returned to these elements when he designed Otis's second house (1800-1802).[3] This severity is directly attributable to the model Bulfinch found in the impressive William Bingham house in Philadelphia which he had visited and sketched in 1789. In Bulfinch's opinion the Bingham house was "in a stile which would be esteemed splendid even in the most luxurious parts of Europe" and "far *too* rich for *any* man in this country."[4] It remains uncertain whether this rather harsh judgment had mellowed somewhat or whether Otis himself had been impressed by the house on business trips to Philadelphia and had requested something similar for his Cambridge Street house.

In any event, the elevation that Bulfinch made for the Otis house closely resembles the drawing he made of the Bingham house. As built, however, the Otis house differs from the elevation principally in the treatment of the second-story windows. The interior of the Otis house was a full-blown expression of the Federal style which Bulfinch had introduced to Boston. Otis's ownership of the house parallels his career in national politics, so one may

wonder how much time he actually spent in it. In the spring of 1797, just as he and his wife Sally and their four small children moved in, he went to Philadelphia to serve his first term in Congress. Not until 1801 did he withdraw from Federal politics and return to Boston. The Cambridge Street house was sold to John Osborn, a paint merchant, on April 15, 1801, although it was apparently not until October 1802[5] that the Otises moved into their next house, also designed by Bulfinch, at 85 Mount Vernon Street on the crest of Beacon Hill.[6]

Osborn put the Cambridge Street house up for sale in 1807, at which time the Boston directory listed his residence as Olive Street, indicating that he too had moved to the already more fashionable residential area on Beacon Hill. The year before, Otis had moved into his third and largest house, again designed by Bulfinch, at 45 Beacon Street, where he remained until his death in 1848.

Failing to sell the Cambridge Street house, Osborn moved back into it in 1816. The inventory of his estate made in October 1819 and an auction notice in the *Columbian Centinel* for May 14, 1823, listed gilded chairs, Grecian card tables, and large looking glasses, indicating that the house was still elegantly furnished. When his daughter moved out of the house and sold the property in 1823, the house was divided through the middle, and interior partitions were installed—the only major alterations ever made. During the remainder of the 1820's the south-

Fig. 3. The earliest known view of the Otis house appeared as the frontispiece of *The Ladies' Medical Oracle; or, Mrs. Mott's Advice to Young Females, Wives, and Mothers* (Boston, 1834). The semicircular porch and the shutters at the windows were probably added during the alterations of 1823. *Society for the Preservation of New England Antiquities.*

Fig. 4. Parlor as it appeared in 1926 when it was used by the SPNEA as exhibition space. Among other relics on display are a decanter and glasses which belonged to Mrs. Harrison Gray Otis. *SPNEA.*

east portion of the newly divided house was occupied by Stillman Lothrop, the looking-glass maker.

On June 28, 1834, the *Daily Evening Transcript* announced that the house had been rented by a Mr. and Mrs. Williams in conjunction with Dr. and Mrs. Mott, "the celebrated Female Physician" for a "Select Establishment for invalid ladies and gentlemen with their Wives." In that year Mrs. Mott published a book whose frontispiece was a woodcut showing the exterior of the house (Fig. 3).

The building later became a rooming house in the gently decaying West End, and that was its function when it was purchased in 1916 as the headquarters of the Society for the Preservation of New England Antiquities. Work started almost immediately to'restore the rooms to their original proportions and replace missing elements of the composition and plasterwork. At first, only the second-floor withdrawing room was furnished to reflect the Otis period. The third-floor rooms were converted to office space and those on the first floor housed the Society's growing collections (Fig. 4).

When Cambridge Street was widened in 1926 the house was moved back forty feet and connected to two 1840 row houses. The expanded exhibition space allowed the Society to restore all the rooms on the first two floors of the Otis House as a historic house museum and to display in them the Society's best pieces of furniture.

The current refurbishing project began in 1970. One of its main purposes was to restore the walls and floors as

accurately as possible to their original appearance. The results were unforeseen and are somewhat surprising in terms of what is commonly thought of as being typically Federal.

Choosing wallpapers was relatively simple, for samples of several of the original papers had been preserved under subsequent layers. In 1916 all layers of paper had been removed and separated and their room location and location in the sequence carefully noted. The layer of paper next to the plaster in most cases bore an English tax stamp which indicated a date in the 1790's and clearly established Otis's preference for small-figure, imported papers in an urban market which was known to offer a wide variety of choices. These papers and their borders have been reproduced. Since no samples of wallpaper survived in either the parlor or the dining room, the decision was made to use plain papers

Overleaf.
Pl. II. Parlor (see also Fig. 4). The original mantel was more like the one in the dining room (see Fig. 5) in scale and ornamentation. Over the replacement hangs a portrait of Mrs. Nathaniel Otis, a cousin of Harrison Gray Otis, painted by John Johnston (1753-1818) in 1801. Two of the shield-back chairs around the tea table originally belonged to John Hancock. The two other chairs, the tea table, and the settee descended in the Bartlett family of Newburyport.

Fig. 5. Dining room (see also Pl. I). Henry Sargent's painting *The Dinner Party* is the source for the hanging of the curtains, the classical busts over the doors, and the crumb cloth under the table.

with borders because such a treatment was popular during the 1790's (see Pls. I, II, Fig. 5). Those papers and their borders were reproductions of ones originally used at Montpelier, the home of Otis's friend Henry Knox in Thomaston, Maine. That house was designed about 1794, probably by Bulfinch. Samples of papers found in two of the bedrooms of the Otis House were not sufficiently large to establish the complete pattern, so these rooms are papered in patterns of comparable scale found in third-floor bedrooms. In all papers the colors are reproduced in their original intensities.

When Osborn bought the house he at first repapered only two or three rooms. However, during his twenty-year

Preceding page.
Pl. III. Withdrawing room. It was planned as the most elegant in the house. The mahogany doors have mirrors let into the panels, and the original mantel was of imported marble. It was undoubtedly here that Otis hung the best of the seventeenth- and eighteenth-century Flemish paintings he collected. The japanned fancy chairs and matching settee (a corner of which is visible at far right) belonged to Otis. Some of the pieces are on loan from the Museum of Fine Arts, Boston. The silver-plated hot-water urn on the tea tray belonged to Otis; the porcelain tea set descended in the family of his half sister Mary Otis.

ownership he did redecorate the whole house once, probably when he returned in 1816. Under the architectural changes of 1823 were what appeared at first glance to be early French scenic wallpapers. Further study revealed that they were actually landscape murals painted on paper. A comparison of the figures in the remaining fragments of these murals with similar figures in murals painted in 1810 by Michele Felice Cornè in the Sullivan Dorr House in Providence suggests that Cornè may have been employed to decorate part if not all of the Otis house while he was residing in Boston between 1807 and 1822.

Determining the original paint colors for each of the rooms became a major project. Scraping to the first layer revealed muddy colors that did not correspond to those described in contemporary painters' manuals and other documents. More scientific techniques revealed that some bright pigments had faded and that glazes used to give the paint a glossy finish had turned brownish-yellow with age. Samples taken from places where the paint was thickest were analyzed chemically and microscopically. The old paints were then duplicated in texture as well as color. Most rooms were painted with variations of a light bluish-green color. Composition ornaments in both the dining room and parlor were picked out in white (see Pl. V), while the doors, baseboards, chair rails, and mantel shelves in these rooms were grained to imitate mahogany; only the second-floor withdrawing room (Pl. III) had real mahogany doors.

Fig. 6. This small first-floor room probably served both as a library and home office. The safe with iron doors over the right-hand half of the mantel is balanced with false doors on the left. The mid-eighteenth-century hatchment descended in the Willard family of Cambridge. The chair, possibly made in Boston, is from the office of the third Harrison Gray Otis House on Beacon Street.

Fig. 7. Front entry. Inventories of the period indicate that dining tables were placed in the entry when not in use. John Hancock's inventory of 1794 relates that his entry of comparable size was hung with twenty-four paintings and seventy prints ''framed and unframed.''

Pl. IV. Ell chamber (see also Fig. 9). The mahogany bed with birch inlay on the foot posts and a painted cornice descended in the Goddard family of Brookline. (A similar one appears in Charles F. Montgomery, *American Furniture: The Federal Period*, New York, 1966, Fig. 1). The wing chair was bought at a sale of the contents of the Beacon Street house in 1889. The prints over the mantelpiece all have a history of ownership in New England before 1820. The carpet is similar in design to one depicted in John (or Johann) Eckstein's (c. 1736-1817) painting of the Samels family of Philadelphia done in 1788 and now in the Museum of Fine Arts, Boston.

The surface treatments produced when the excellently documented Otis and Osborn interiors were restored reveal combinations of colors that may seem somewhat discordant to modern taste. Their veracity is corroborated, however, by contemporary pictorial sources which serve as a stern reminder that Federal taste in design and color is not necessarily ours today.

The house was furnished to produce a composite of Boston's taste during the Federal period since not enough is known to reflect either the Otis or the Osborn occupancy alone. The year 1820 was chosen as a cutoff date, and objects used by both owners took priority in establishing the scale of elegance to be shown. These surviving items were coordinated with research into the inventories of comparable estates in Boston, and diary references to other houses of the same caliber, especially houses designed by Bulfinch or occupied by friends of Otis. The Society's collections were culled for additional pieces of furniture and decorative accessories of the period with appropriate

Pl. V. Central tablet of the dining room mantel (see Fig. 5). Elaborate composition ornaments such as this, called stuccowork, decorate the woodwork in the major rooms of the house. Following the precedent set by the Adam brothers, the ornaments are picked out in contrasting colors. Identical ornaments have been found on English and American looking glasses of the period.

Pl. VI. Miniature of Mrs. Harrison Gray Otis (1770-1836) by Edward Greene Malbone (1777-1836); 1804. Their correspondence shows that Sally Foster Otis and her husband were devoted to each other for the forty-six years of their married life. This miniature was presented to the Society by Mrs. Otis's granddaughter. The carnelian cross set with pearls and a topaz that Mrs. Otis is wearing descended in another branch of the family and is also now owned by the Society.

Fig. 8. Back stair. This provides the only access to the third floor. The paper, a copy of the second layer found on the walls, was a popular pattern in New England and has been found in a variety of colors. This space was papered both by Otis and Osborn, whereas the walls of the front entry were painted from the outset.

Fig. 9. Ell chamber (see also Pl. IV). The small blockfront chest of drawers and the mirror stand, both c. 1750, belonged to Otis's half sister Mary Otis, who perhaps inherited them from her parents.

provenance, and Osborn's inventory of 1819 was used as a guide for the quantity of furniture in each room. Paintings and prints were used to determine the placement of furnishings within a room, the window treatments, and the designs for the reproduction carpeting. Evidence for laying the carpet wall to wall was found both in contemporary pictures and in the house itself where removal of the later Victorian carpets in 1916 revealed floors made up in most cases of narrow widths of soft pine, rough and unpainted.

Perhaps the two most useful pictorial sources consulted were paintings by Henry Sargent (1770-1845) entitled *The Tea Party*[7] and *The Dinner Party* now at the Museum of Fine Arts in Boston. Although they were painted just after the time period covered in the restoration, they are important as the only early nineteenth-century illustrations of Boston interiors and, happily, they depict rooms in houses designed by Charles Bulfinch.

The interiors of the Otis house are not intended to remain static. As more pieces associated with Otis and Osborn turn up and scholarship contributes new insights into the original furnishings, it is hoped that the house will reflect with increasing accuracy the Federal period in Boston.

Fig. 10. Middle chamber, adjoining the withdrawing room on the second floor. It is furnished according to the Osborn inventory with only a bed, washstand, and chest of drawers. Straw matting was a common floor covering in secondary rooms. The bed hangings are modeled on a set of c. 1810 in the SPNEA collection and are fashioned from a reproduction of an English chintz of c. 1812.

[1] The life of each of these men is best described in the following books: Harold Kirker, *The Architecture of Charles Bulfinch* (Cambridge, 1969), and Samuel Eliot Morison, *Harrison Gray Otis, 1765-1848: The Urbane Federalist* (Boston, 1969).

[2] Henry Wansey, *The Journal of an Excursion to the United States of North America in the Summer of 1794* (Salisbury, 1796), p. 39.

[3] See ANTIQUES, October 1967, pp. 536-541.

[4] Ellen Susan Bulfinch, *The Life and Letters of Charles Bulfinch, Architect* (Boston, 1896), pp. 75-76, as quoted in Kirker, *Architecture of Charles Bulfinch*, p. 119. The Bingham house, in turn, was a larger copy of the Duke of Manchester's house in London which today, in a much modified form, houses the Wallace Collection.

[5] William Foster, Mrs. Otis's father, noted in a daybook on October 7, 1802:

"Mr. & Mrs. Otis went to ther New House with the family & Lodged first time." The daybook is in a private collection.

[6] In addition to designing that house, Bulfinch was also laying out streets for a new development on the eighteen acres of pasture on Beacon Hill which the Mount Vernon Proprietors bought from John Singleton Copley in 1796. Otis, as an incorporator of the Proprietors, foresaw that the location of the new statehouse on Beacon Hill in 1795 would make the Copley land desirable as a residential district. Each proprietor built a house on it (Otis's being at 85 Mount Vernon Street), thus establishing the architectural tone. Indeed, it appears from Mrs. Otis's inscription on the Bulfinch elevation for the Cambridge Street house (Fig. 2) that that house was intended for the Mount Vernon Street location.

[7] A detail appeared on the cover of ANTIQUES for November 1974.

Living with antiques

The Southern furniture collection of Mr. and Mrs. William C. Adams Jr.

BY ELIZABETH TAYLOR CHILDS
Curator, department of collections, Valentine Museum

WHILE COLLECTORS in the 1950's were choosing sophisticated English and American furnishings, Mr. and Mrs. William C. Adams Jr. of Richmond were searching Virginia for simpler examples of country cabinetmaking. As a result, they have one of the finest private collections of Southern furniture in the South. Although their greatest love is for Virginia-made furniture, they have collected pieces made in all parts of the South before 1830. The Adamses' interest goes beyond simply collecting, for they welcome serious scholars who wish to examine individual pieces of their furniture more closely.

Their house is a brick, gambrel-roof copy of an eighteenth-century Tidewater Virginia merchant's house. All the floors, mantels, and door locks are from late eighteenth- and early nineteenth-century Virginia houses.

At the far end of the Adamses' entrance hall is a simple stretcher table of c. 1720 from southeastern Virginia or northeastern North Carolina. It is made of walnut, with yellow pine the secondary wood; the skirt and box stretcher are made from walnut more than an inch thick. The heavy construction is an indication of its rural origin. The walnut gateleg table of c. 1720 to the right was found in Louisa County, Virginia. Above it hangs an early eighteenth-century portrait of a New England clergyman by an unknown artist. The banister-back side chair with fishtail crest is one of a pair believed to have been made in New England c. 1740, which retain their original red paint. The rug is Kurdish. *Photographs are by Helga Photo Studio.*

In the library is a superb desk-and-bookcase of the mid-eighteenth century. Found in southeastern Virginia, it is of cherry, with oak and yellow pine the secondary woods. The meticulous execution of the interior details and drawers is characteristic of much Tidewater furniture; similar attention to detail is found in fine English furniture of the eighteenth century. On the desk is a polychrome wood figure of a militiaman thought to have been made in the Valley of Virginia in the early nineteenth century. Drawn up to the desk is a Pennsylvania bow-back windsor chair of c. 1750. Above the William and Mary daybed of c. 1700 is a Virginia hanging cupboard of walnut, made c. 1750. The Pennsylvania slat-back armchair in the foreground was made between 1720 and 1750.

The parlor extends the full depth of the house. A walnut desk-and-bookcase of c. 1790 dominates the room. It has been attributed to the Winchester, Virginia, region by Wallace Gusler. Another desk-and-bookcase, two high chests of drawers, and a corner cupboard from the same school of cabinetmaking are in the collection at Colonial Williamsburg. In front of the desk-and-bookcase is one of a set of four walnut side chairs made in Virginia between 1760 and 1810. Beneath the Pennsylvania Chippendale looking glass of c. 1780 stands a Maryland side chair of c. 1810. The mahogany sofa at the right has heavy, yellow-pine seat rails, braces, and front corner blocks. It is Southern and dates from c. 1810. The mahogany pembroke table of 1780–1790 at the end of the sofa was found in Fredericksburg, Virginia. The mahogany pembroke table in front of the sofa is of Maryland origin, c. 1790. The painting above the sofa is a nineteenth-century copy of *The Woodland Gate*, by William Collins (1788–1847), which was exhibited at the Royal Academy in London in 1836. The serpentine sofa at the left is probably from Philadelphia, c. 1760. It has blind-fretwork legs and pierced stretchers.

The cherry hanging corner cupboard of c. 1780 in the parlor was found in Fauquier County, Virginia. Inside it is a collection of China Trade porcelain. The mahogany Queen Anne tea table has a history of ownership that strongly suggests it was made in Middlesex County, Virginia, c. 1740. Flanking the tea table are two more of the Virginia side chairs mentioned in the preceding caption. Beside the American Queen Anne roundabout chair of c. 1730 is a simple candlestand of c. 1790 that has a cherry top and legs and a walnut column. It is also attributed to Virginia owing to a strong Virginia family history. The rug is an extremely large Heriz.

The mahogany high-post bed dominates the Adamses' bedroom. They acquired it from the Caroline County, Virginia, family for whom it was made c. 1775. The bed hangings were worked by Mrs. Adams in crewels on linen mainly in Roumanian couching and flat stitches. The tilt-top mahogany table beside the bed was made in Newport c. 1780. On it is a flask of c. 1770 decorated with Stiegel-type engraving of baskets of flowers. The walnut high chest of drawers from Chester County, Pennsylvania, was made 1760–1780. It has burl-walnut drawer fronts, and poplar is the secondary wood. At the foot of the bed is a walnut blanket chest of c. 1725 with cotter-pin hinges. The Adamses found this chest in Petersburg, Virginia. On it rest a weathered carved eagle said to have been taken from the bridge of a ship, and a Jacquard-weave coverlet.

In the upstairs hall stands this walnut chest on frame, c. 1790, made in Mecklenburg County, North Carolina. The red leather brass-studded dispatch box is English, c. 1800. The brass chamber candlestick was probably made in England in the late eighteenth century. An anonymous artist painted the portrait of an unknown woman c. 1850.

In the niche on the staircase landing stands a mahogany pillar-and-scroll clock with the label of Eli Terry and Sons (w. 1818–1824) of Plymouth, Connecticut. The pair of American mahogany looking glasses was made c. 1820. On the simple maple candlestand of New England origin stand a nineteenth-century leather key basket and an English brass candlestick, c. 1750.

Adjoining the kitchen is a breakfast room with an open hearth that is frequently used for roasting. An English eighteenth-century oak dresser holds a collection of American and English pewter. The oak gateleg table of c. 1700 was found between Culpeper and Fredericksburg, and has a history of ownership in Virginia. The pair of Delaware valley ladder-back chairs was made between 1720 and 1750. The bow-back windsor armchair at the far side of the table is from Delaware, c. 1790. It is branded S. BARNET, for Sampson Barnet, who advertised in the *Delaware Gazette, and General Advertiser* on October 31, 1789. The Pennsylvania chestnut and pine settle of c. 1800 retains its original red paint. The painting is an 1887 copy of Richard Norris Brooke's (1847–1920) *A Pastoral Visit– The Minister Comes to Dinner*, of 1886. It is inscribed at lower right, *after Richard N. Brooke, Grey 1887*.

The walnut table in the dining room is attributed to the Valley of Virginia, c. 1800. It has drop-leaf ends. Around the table are walnut Chippendale chairs of Southern origin, made c. 1775. The corner cupboard of walnut and yellow pine, c. 1800, has its original glass and hardware. It was found in Dinwiddie County, Virginia. To the left of the corner cupboard is an exceptionally fine Queen Anne walnut drop-leaf table of c. 1740 from Virginia. The silver teapot, creamer, and sugar bowl are marked T. FLETCHER/PHILAD. and inscribed *Rose Nelson from her parents and grandma*. Thomas Fletcher (1787–1866) used the mark found on these pieces between c. 1825 and 1842. The nineteenth-century painting above the table depicts a minuteman being called to arms.

In this corner of the dining room is a walnut serving table which has a top with a molded edge and five-sided, beaded legs. It was found in Fredericksburg, Virginia, by the present owners. On it are a pair of China Trade covered dishes in the Canton pattern and a silver ladle with shell-pattern handle marked by Taylor and Hinsdale of New York City. The Southern walnut high chair of c. 1780 still retains its original cornhusk seat.

Marie Marshall of Savannah, Georgia, artist unknown, c. 1810. Oil on canvas, 46 by 36 inches. The sitter was a member of a prominent Savannah family and is buried in Bonaventure Cemetery there. A portrait of Marie in her late thirties, signed *Peter Laurens/Savannah,* is in a private collection in Savannah.

In this guest bedroom is a Virginia walnut clothes press, c. 1775, with paneled doors and the original drawer pulls. Beneath the portrait of an unidentified lady in a lace bonnet is an Orange County, Virginia, blanket chest of c. 1780. In the foreground is a Southern table of pine made c. 1790. The skirt is cut into an arch on all four sides for the convenience of those seated at the table.

This bedroom contains a varied collection of miniature furniture and toys. Of special interest is the miniature mahogany bed, c. 1830, with its delicately carved posts which incorporate spirals as well as acanthus leaves and pineapple motifs. The pieced quilt of c. 1830 on the canopied curly-maple bed is done in an eight-pointed-star motif. Beside the bed is a New England tavern table of c. 1720. The 1780's blanket chest of walnut and yellow pine was found by the present owners in Charlotte County, Virginia. The painting above it, by an unknown artist, is dated 1822.

One of the most important objects in the Adamses' collection is the desk-and-bookcase in their bedroom. It is made of walnut, with yellow pine and oak the secondary woods. Wallace Gusler has attributed it to Peter Scott (1694–1775) of Williamsburg. It is identical in construction and decoration to several pieces of case furniture linked to Scott. In 1784 Colonel William Bassett of New Kent County, Virginia, recorded in his account book a payment of £5 to Scott for a desk. It is perhaps the desk shown here, which was sold about seventy-five years ago at the dispersal sale of Cloverlea in Hanover, Virginia, one of the Bassett family houses. Still remaining with the desk-and-bookcase is a box marked *Bassett* which contains architect's instruments. At the desk-and-bookcase is a Virginia walnut chair with tapered splat of c. 1780. The walnut chest of drawers of c. 1725 was found in Fredericksburg, Virginia. It has walnut ball feet doweled into yellow-pine cleats. On top of the chest is a fancy medicine box of c. 1830 painted to imitate burl wood. Attributed to the Valley of Virginia, the box is inscribed *David Gelvnick his/he painted it.*

The walnut side table of c. 1775 in this corner of the parlor is a Southern provincial adaptation of a sophisticated English form. The mid-eighteenth-century English brass candlesticks flank a China Trade porcelain punch bowl. Above the side table is a late nineteenth-century interpretation of Eastman Johnson's (1824–1906) *Barefoot Boy.* The Virginia walnut side chair of 1760–1810 is especially interesting for the heart motif in its pierced splat. A Southern chair with a similar splat is illustrated in John T. Kirk, *American Chairs: Queen Anne and Chippendale* (New York, 1972, p. 158, Fig. 216). The mahogany demilune card table, c. 1800, has the same inlaid flower paterae as the Baltimore cupboard illustrated in Charles F. Montgomery, *American Furniture, The Federal Period* (New York, 1966, No. 444).

Living with antiques

The Hays-Kiser house, Antioch, Tennessee

BY JOHN KISER

ACCORDING TO family tradition, Charles Hays (1777-1854) built the house shown in Plate I in Antioch, Tennessee, about ten miles southeast of Nashville, sometime before he married Anna Blackman in 1795. Hays bought the land from white settlers, but he is said to have purchased safety from attack by the Indians by paying them six horses and ten bags of salt for all the land visible (2500 acres) from the hilltop site of the house. He is also said to have employed men to build the house whom his father, John Hays, brought with him from Sampson County, North Carolina, for the purpose. The house is still sometimes referred to locally as "the old North Carolina house."

An English visitor to Nashville in 1797 noted that the buildings there were "chiefly frame and log,"* indicating that Hays' house, built of bricks made on the site, was a rarity in the region at the time. During the next twenty-five years a number of other brick houses similar in size and plan to Hays' house were built in Davidson County, but few survive today. The Hays-Kiser house is thought to be the oldest brick house still standing in the county.

In plan the house resembles other houses of the period in Kentucky, Virginia, and North Carolina. The front door opens directly into the larger of the two rooms that make up the first floor of the main block (see Fig. 3). A stairway leads from the smaller room to the second floor, where the plan is repeated. The larger of the two upstairs rooms

*Francis Baily, quoted in H. W. Crew, *History of Nashville* (Nashville, 1890), p. 94.

(frontispiece) has a poplar-paneled fireplace wall which is the most elaborate in the house and has fortunately never been repainted. This grand room, now a bedroom, may represent a holdover from the practice common on the east coast of the Carolinas in the eighteenth century of having a drawing room on the second floor.

Connected to the smaller room on the first floor is an ell that originally consisted of one room and was one story high. Sometime after the house was built, a one-room second story, known by family tradition as the "boy's room," was added to the ell. The upstairs room was accessible only from the gallery of a two-story porch that was probably added at the same time. The porch was removed around the beginning of the twentieth century, but after my wife and I bought the house in 1966 we found what appears to be one of its original columns in an outbuilding on the property.

In 1870 the house and part of the surrounding farm were bought by the Rieves family, who lived there until 1965. During their occupancy they demolished the original separate dining room and kitchen and enlarged the ell so that it extended the full width of the house. The new two-story addition comprised an inside kitchen and dining area on the first floor and a bedroom on the second. In 1894 they added a two-story porch across the front of the house which so changed the appearance of the façade that the house was advertised for sale in 1966 as "a 175 years old Victorian house," an ambiguity of phrasing that piqued our curiosity.

Fig. 1. Detail of the mantel in what is now the living room (Pl. II). Fragments found outside the house raise the interesting possibility that the fireplace may once have been faced with green marble. *Photographs are by Helga Photo Studio.*

Pl. I. Hays-Kiser house, Antioch, Davidson County, Tennessee, built by Charles Hays c. 1795. The bricks are laid in Flemish bond on a cut-limestone foundation. When we bought the house in 1966 the fine brickwork of the exterior was painted red and a two-story Victorian porch spanned the front façade. Some of the original nine-over-nine-pane windows had been replaced by two-over-two-pane windows, and the shutters and many of the wrought-iron latches which hold the shutters against the wall were gone. Fortunately, a local craftsman was able to duplicate the missing latches from surviving ones. The house was listed in the National Register of Historic Places in 1974 and in the Historic American Buildings Survey in 1971.

When we bought the house we discovered that the original staircase had been removed and some of the original doorways had been closed off. Some of the doors turned up in an outbuilding and have now been rehung in their original places. We also found the outline of the original staircase, including the balusters and handrail, under layers of wallpaper, and it has been reconstructed accordingly. The original colors of the woodwork, which is local poplar throughout the house, were determined by the careful removal of several layers of paint, and those colors have been duplicated in each room. We have selected furnishings for the house that date from between about 1795 and 1854, the years Charles Hays lived in the house. Hays' inventories of 1847 and 1854 suggest handsome furnishings in keeping with the architecture of the house but, unfortunately, except for a portrait of his granddaughter (see Fig. 3), none of his furnishings have been found.

Fig. 2. This side porch was constructed from lumber which remained after the demolition of a long gallery with louvered sides that connected the house to the original separate kitchen and dining room. To the left is the ell.

Fig. 3. The front door leads directly into the living room. To the left of the door is a mahogany Empire card table of c. 1830, above which hangs a copy of a posthumous portrait of Maria Louisa Hays, granddaughter of the builder of the house, who died at the age of four. The original, painted in 1841, is now in the collection of a descendant of Charles Hays. According to the subject's grandniece, it was painted by an artist known only as having been "in Nashville to paint General Jackson." Both sofas were made in Philadelphia c. 1835.

Pl. II. The fireplace surround in the larger of the two rooms on the first floor of the main house is carved in a manner associated with Germanic craftsmen (see Fig. 1). Some of the motifs are repeated in the carving on the chair rail. The woodwork in this room and throughout the house is native poplar, which is light in weight and easy to work, and was abundant in Tennessee when the house was built. The Federal table of c. 1790 in front of the window is mahogany inlaid in a manner which suggests a Baltimore origin. The looking glass that hangs above the English oak Queen Anne drop-leaf table of c. 1750 was made in Germany in the late eighteenth century. The klismos chair dates from c. 1820. The Sheraton sewing basket is English, c. 1800.

Fig. 4. The dining-room mantel is painted its original dark green and the rest of the woodwork the original soft gray. Rose Medallion porcelain adorns the mantel and the modern drop-leaf table. On the floor is an ingrain carpet of c. 1835. To the right of the fireplace is one of two miniatures of Andrew Jackson by Ralph E. W. Earl (c. 1788-1838) in our collection.

Decorative arts at the White House

BY CLEMENT E. CONGER, *Curator*

Pl. I. The Library was furnished in the Federal style during
the Kennedy administration (1961–1963) and refurbished in
1976. Much of the furniture is thought to have been made
in New York City between 1800 and 1820. The New York
mahogany side chairs flanking the door are attributed to
the shop of Duncan Phyfe (1768–1854), c. 1810, and match
the armchair shown at the right in Pl. III. The caned settee
(one of a pair) and the eight lattice-back chairs in the room
are also attributed to Phyfe's shop. Above the settee hangs
a gilded looking glass possibly made in New York,
1800–1810, which is decorated with an *églomisé* panel bearing an American eagle holding a banner inscribed *E Pluribus
Unum*. The paintings of American Indians who visited the
White House in 1822 are by Charles Bird King.

Pl. II. Mixing table labeled underneath the top by
Charles-Honoré Lannuier (1779–1819), New York
City, 1810–1815. Mahogany and green Pennsylvania
marble; height 28¼, width 23¾, depth 16¼ inches. The
table is partly visible at the right in the view of the
Library shown in Pl. I.

Pl. III. The handsome mantel in the Library was carved by Samuel McIntire (1757–1811) of Salem, Massachusetts, 1795–1805. The late eighteenth-century English silver Argand lamps on it are believed to have been presented to General Henry Knox, the first secretary of war, by the marquis de Lafayette. Above the mantel hangs an Athenaeum-type portrait of George Washington (1732–1799) by Gilbert Stuart (1755–1828). The mahogany armchair at the left of the fireplace was made in Massachusetts, 1800–1810; that on the right is attributed to Phyfe's shop (see also Pl. I).

IN MARCH 1792 Thomas Jefferson instructed the commissioners of public buildings to hold competitions and offer premiums for the design of the Capitol and the President's House to be built in the District of Columbia. The commissioners offered a prize of $500 or a medal of that value for the winning design for the President's House. A number of plans were submitted, including one by Jefferson, who signed himself simply *A. Z.* George Washington chose the design of James Hoban, an Irish-born architect living in South Carolina, for a simple Palladian building modeled on Leinster House in Dublin, now the Irish National Parliament. Washington supervised the building of the President's House, but he was out of office and had died before it was finished.

John Adams, the first resident president, moved into the house on November 1, 1800, when it was still unfurnished and unheated. The building was sacked and set on fire by the British on August 24, 1814, during the War of 1812, and only the exterior walls survived. Hoban was hired to rebuild the house, which reopened in 1817, during the administration of James Monroe.

Pl. IV. Lighthouse clock made by Simon Willard and Sons, Roxbury, Massachusetts, c. 1825. Mahogany and brass; height 29½ inches. Willard patented the Eddystone Lighthouse Alarm Timepiece in 1822, but this example was probably made about the time Lafayette made his triumphal return to the United States in 1824 and 1825, to judge by the commemorative sulphide portrait of the French soldier and statesman on the base. The clock is now in the Library (see Pl. III).

Pl. V. On display in the Vermeil Room is much of the fine collection of silver gilt bequeathed to the White House by Margaret Thompson Biddle of Philadelphia in 1956. Most of the objects in the collection were made in England and France in the eighteenth and nineteenth centuries. The American mahogany pier table of 1810–1815, at the left, is on loan from the Metropolitan Museum of Art. Above it hangs a portrait of Eleanor Roosevelt (1884–1962) painted by Douglas Chandor (1897–1953) in 1949. The marble-topped mahogany center table with gilt-bronze mounts is one of the many French furnishings James Monroe acquired in 1817 for the White House, which had just been rebuilt after the British burned it during the War of 1812. The French marble mantel of c. 1830 is flanked by a pair of early nineteenth-century mahogany settees made in Massachusetts. Above the mantel hangs *Morning on the Seine*, painted in 1897 by Claude Monet (1840–1926) and given to the White House by the Kennedy family in memory of John F. Kennedy. The wool and silk Turkish rug was woven at the Hereke factory near Istanbul.

Pl. VI. Card table attributed to Lannuier, New York City, 1810–1815. Mahogany and brass; height 30½, width 36¾, depth (closed) 18⅛ inches. The table was part of the original furnishings of Point Breeze, Joseph Bonaparte's estate in Bordentown, New Jersey. It is attributed to Lannuier on the basis of its similarity to a labeled table now on loan to the White House. Both tables and a pair of similar tables, also attributed to Lannuier, are used in the Vermeil Room (Pl. V).

The interiors have been constantly altered as styles have changed. In 1902, under President Theodore Roosevelt, the Victorian décor of the late nineteenth century was stripped away and the interior was completely redecorated by the New York firm of McKim, Mead and White, who at the same time designed and constructed the West Wing to house the offices of the president and his staff (see Pls. XIII, XIV). The West Wing was enlarged in 1909, in 1927, and again in 1934, and the East Wing, also devoted to offices, was erected in 1942. The last major renovation took place between 1948 and 1952 under President Harry S. Truman. The Army Corps of Engineers made the building structurally sound and fireproofed and air-conditioned it, but unfortunately most of the early architectural trim and plaster ornament was cut into pieces and sold or given away as souvenirs. Mantels and chandeliers were given away to institutions throughout the country, and the wooden floors and plaster walls in the main corridors on the ground and second floors were replaced with an overabundance of marble.

Pl. VII. The China Room was created in 1917 to display the collection of presidential porcelain begun in 1889 by Mrs. Benjamin Harrison and enlarged by later presidents' wives. Above the early nineteenth-century French marble mantel hangs *View on the Mississippi, Fifty-Seven Miles Below St. Anthony Falls, Minneapolis*, painted by Ferdinand Reichardt (1819–1895) in 1858, the year Minnesota became the thirty-second state. On the floor is a mid-nineteenth-century Axminster carpet.

Pl. VIII. Diplomatic Reception Room on the ground floor. An unusual feature of James Hoban's design is the series of three oval rooms located directly above one another which project into the bay on the south façade of the White House. Above the oval Diplomatic Reception Room are the Blue Room (Pl. XXXVIII), on the second floor, and the Yellow Oval Room (Pls. XXV, XXVI), on the third floor. The Diplomatic Reception Room was furnished as a Federal-style drawing room in 1960, during the Eisenhower administration. The wallpaper, entitled *Scenic America*, was first block printed in Rixheim, Alsace, France, by Jean Zuber et Cie in 1834 and depicts the Natural Bridge of Virginia, Niagara Falls, West Point, New York Bay, Boston Harbor, and Winnebago Indians dancing. At the left is a mahogany tall-case clock made by Effingham Embree (w. 1789–1796) of New York. The mahogany desk-and-bookcase of 1797 is labeled by John Shaw (1745–1829) of Annapolis, Maryland. The early nineteenth-century settee beside it is one of a pair in the room attributed to Abraham Slover and Jacob Taylor, who worked together in New York between 1802 and 1805.

Pl. IX. The Map Room is so called because it was here that Franklin D. Roosevelt, Winston Churchill, and other foreign dignitaries met to study maps of the theaters of action during World War II. In 1970 it was redesigned as a drawing room in the Chippendale style. The Chinese Chippendale mahogany side table was made in Philadelphia, 1770–1775. The mahogany chair to the right of it is believed to be the only known labeled piece by James Gillingham (see Pl. X) of Philadelphia, but several of the other chairs in the room are attributed to him. In the corner is a mahogany block-front desk of 1760–1775 with carved shells characteristic of furniture made by the Townsend-Goddard school of Newport, Rhode Island. The desk, on loan from the Dietrich Corporation, is flanked by a pair of late eighteenth-century Philadelphia mahogany side chairs that belonged to George Washington when the president's residence was in Philadelphia. They are on loan from the Barra Foundation, Incorporated. Above the desk hangs a portrait of Benjamin Franklin (1706–1790) painted in 1759 by Benjamin Wilson (1721–1788), an English artist and man of science. Over the mantel hangs Albert Bierstadt's (1830–1902) *Autumn Landscape*, which is on loan from Elizabeth Wilson Fleming. The English cut-glass chandelier of 1760–1770 has unusual star pendants. The late nineteenth-century rug is from Herez in western Iran. The inappropriate marble floor, mantel, and other architectural details date from the Truman renovation.

Pl. X. Side chair labeled by James Gillingham (1736–1781), Philadelphia, 1760–1770. Mahogany; height 38¾, width 23½, depth 18½ inches. (See also Pl. IX.)

Pl. XI.   The mahogany sofa with Marlborough legs of c. 1760 in the Map Room was made in New York, as was the rare mahogany tea table, 1760–1780. Above the sofa hangs *Lake Among the Hills*, painted in 1858 by William M. Hart (1823–1894). To its right is a 1755 French edition of a 1751 map of Maryland and Virginia drawn by Joshua Fry and Peter Jefferson, Thomas Jefferson's father. Below the map is a mahogany drop-leaf table made in Newport, 1760–1770. The mahogany tall-case clock in the corner was made by Emanuel Rouse (w. 1747–1768) of Philadelphia c. 1750.

In the past twenty-eight years a concentrated effort has been made to restore the White House to its era of elegance in the early nineteenth century. Mrs. Dwight D. Eisenhower, with the assistance of the National Society of Interior Designers, began the first major effort to establish a permanent collection of antique American furnishings for the White House, but she confined her efforts to the Diplomatic Reception Room (see Pl. VIII). Between 1961 and 1963 Mrs. John F. Kennedy and Henry Francis du Pont directed a major acquisition program to furnish the other rooms with antiques, but despite their notable achievements, at the end of the Kennedy administra-

Pl. XII.   Armchair, one of a pair, New York, 1760–1770. Mahogany; height 38, width 23, depth 22 inches. The armrests end in unusual eagle's-head terminals. The chairs descended in the family of Eleanora Wayles Randolph, a granddaughter of Thomas Jefferson, and are presently used in the Map Room (Pls. IX, XI).

Pl. XIII. The president's Oval Office is in the West Wing, which was begun in 1902 and enlarged in 1909, 1927, and 1934. The tall-case clock was made by John and Thomas Seymour (w. together 1794–c. 1803) of Boston c. 1800 and houses works possibly made by James Doull (w. 1790–1849) of Charlestown, Massachusetts. The portrait of George Washington was painted by Charles Willson Peale (1741–1827) in 1776, and is on loan from Mrs. Lansdell K. Christie. To the left of it hangs George Cooke's (1793–1849) *City of Washington, 1833 From Beyond the Navy Yard*, from which William James Bennett executed a famous engraving of the city. To the right is *Eastport, and Passamaquoddy Bay*, attributed to Victor de Grailly (1804–1889), c. 1845.

Pl. XIV. In the president's Oval Office is a rare mahogany card table with a gilded eagle pedestal made in Salem, Massachusetts, c. 1810. On it stands Frederic Remington's (1861–1909) *Broncho Buster*, cast c. 1901 by the Roman Bronze Works of Corona, New York. The somewhat fanciful depiction of the White House above the bronze was painted by an unknown mid-nineteenth-century artist after William Bartlett's 1839 drawing. The modern rug was designed especially for the room.

Pl. XV. This sitting room for guests of the president and his family is at the east end of the third story. The floor is at this curious level with respect to the window because of the high ceiling of the East Room below (see Pl. XL). On either side of the sitting room are bedroom suites. The mahogany easy chair on the left was made in Massachusetts c. 1795; the mahogany and satinwood lolling chair of 1800–1810 was probably made in Portsmouth, New Hampshire. The English cut-glass chandelier dates from the late eighteenth century; the Tabriz rug, from northwestern Iran, from the late nineteenth or early twentieth century.

Pl. XVI. Bracket clock made by Thomas Pearsall and Effingham Embree, New York City, 1785–1795. Mahogany and brass, with a silver dial; height 21, width 11½, depth 8 inches. This rare American example of an English form is used in the sitting room shown in Pl. XV.

Pl. XVII. Five queens have been among the many distinguished guests to occupy this bedroom, now known as the Queens' Bedroom. The room, to the left of the sitting room shown in Pl. XV, was used by the president's staff until the executive offices were moved to the West Wing in 1902. The mahogany high-post bed of c. 1830 was purchased at a sale of furnishings from the Hermitage, Andrew Jackson's house outside Nashville, Tennessee. The mahogany window seat at the foot of the bed was made in Massachusetts, 1810–1815. The late eighteenth-century cut-glass chandelier is English.

Pl. XVIII. Desk-and-bookcase attributed to John and Thomas Seymour, Boston, c. 1800. Mahogany and curly maple; height 81⅜, width 36⅝, depth 19½ inches. The *églomisé* panels at the base of the doors are decorated with Gothic arches. Behind the tambour doors are drawers and pigeonholes lined with blue paper—a characteristic of the Seymours' work. The desk-and-bookcase stands in the Queens' Bedroom (Pls. XVII, XIX).

tion only one third of the furnishings in the building were American antiques; two-thirds were still reproductions.

Mrs. Richard M. Nixon continued the search for antique furnishings, and in 1970 she began to replace the upholstery, draperies, and other appointments of the Kennedy era which had worn out. Under her aegis, more work was done to extend and improve the collections of the White House than in any previous administration. Happily, the programs she instituted have been carried forward by the Ford and Carter administrations, with the result that new draperies, upholstery, and furnishings have been installed in twenty-two rooms, most of them restored as authentically as possible to the first quarter of the nineteenth century. Duplicate upholstery and drapery fabrics were ordered, and extra furniture has been acquired so that replacements or substitutions can be made as fabrics wear out, objects are sent out for repair, or furnishings on loan are returned to their owners.

As a result of these efforts, the White House is now more handsomely appointed as a period house than it has ever been in its history. However, with half a dozen exceptions, Congressional appropriations for the White House have provided only for routine maintenance. Acquisitions and major refurbishing efforts are paid for with donations.

Pl. XIX. The mahogany sofa in the Queens' Bedroom was probably made in Salem, 1795–1800. Above it hangs Thomas Sully's portrait of Fanny Kemble (see p. 137, Pl. V), flanked by a pair of English gilded wall brackets, c. 1760, which support a pair of Chinese enameled vases, 1740–1750. On the adjacent wall hangs an 1830 portrait by Ralph E. W. Earl (c. 1788–1838) of Emily Donelson (1807–1836), who served her widower uncle Andrew Jackson as hostess of the White House. The mahogany and bird's-eye-maple chest of drawers of c. 1800 was possibly made in New Hampshire. The Turkish Hereke rug dates from the late nineteenth century.

Pl. XX.   The Lincoln Bedroom is situated to the right of the sitting room shown in Pl. XV. The eight-foot-long rosewood bed and matching marble-topped center table are believed to have been purchased by Mrs. Lincoln in 1861 and were in use in the principal guest bedroom in the White House by 1862. The portrait of Mrs. Lincoln (1818–1882) to the right of the bed was painted from photographs by her niece Katherine Helm (1887–1937) in 1925 and was donated to the White House the following year by Mr. and Mrs. Robert Todd Lincoln. The chest of drawers with full-length mirror has been in the White House since the nineteenth century. The cut-glass chandelier was made in England c. 1860 and was given to the White House because of its resemblance to the chandelier depicted in an engraving of this room when it served as President Lincoln's office and cabinet room.

Pl. XXI.   The walnut slant-front desk of c. 1860 in this corner of the Lincoln Bedroom was used by Lincoln at his summer residence, a cottage on the grounds of the Soldiers' Home in Washington, which was on higher and thus healthier ground than the White House. Drawn up to it is one of four walnut side chairs surviving from a set believed to have been purchased during the administration of James Polk (1845–1849) but used by Lincoln around his cabinet table. On top of the desk is the only one of five holographs of the Gettysburg Address to be signed, dated, and titled by Lincoln. Above the desk hangs William Carlton's (1816–1888) *Watch Meeting/Waiting for the Hour/December 31, 1862*, which depicts slaves and a few friends waiting for midnight, and freedom under the Emancipation Proclamation. The painting was sent to Lincoln by the famous abolitionist William Lloyd Garrison and is believed to have hung in this room. It was later given back to the artist and only in 1972 returned to the White House.

Pl. XXII.   This room, now called the Treaty Room, served as the cabinet room from 1865 until the West Wing was constructed in 1902. It was furnished in 1961 to resemble the cabinet room of President Ulysses S. Grant. The first of many treaties to be signed at the table was the peace protocol of August 1898, signed by President William McKinley, that led to the end of the Spanish-American War. The bentwood swivel armchair was probably used in the cabinet room in the last half of the nineteenth century; the seven walnut chairs are thought to have been purchased during the Polk administration. The gilded looking glass survives from the administration of Franklin Pierce (1853–1857), and the pair of gilt-bronze candelabra, from the inauguration of Andrew Jackson in 1829. The portrait of President Grant (1822–1885) was painted by Henry Ulke (1821–1910) in 1871. The cut-glass English chandelier of c. 1850 is a recent acquisition. The flocked wallpaper and the geometric border are patterned after Victorian designs.

Pl. XXIII. The Center Hall on the third floor serves as a sitting room for the president's family and guests. The rare mahogany chair-back settee and matching armchairs (two of a set of four) were made in Philadelphia c. 1810. To the right are an American mahogany card table of about the same date and a Chinese Coromandel lacquer screen of the K'ang Hsi period (1622–1722). The mahogany card table to the left is one of a pair, 1790–1800, possibly made in New England. On the table is one of a pair of late eighteenth- or early nineteenth-century Chinese porcelain jars; above it hangs a Civil War scene entitled *Seventh Regiment Encamping near Washington*, painted in 1861 by Sanford R. Gifford (1823–1880), which is on loan from the Union League Club of New York.

Pl. XXIV. Looking glass, one of a pair, possibly made in Philadelphia, 1750–1785. Mahogany; height 57, width 32 inches. The looking glasses now hang in the Center Hall (Pl. XXIII). They descended in a Dover, Delaware, family known to have purchased furniture from the cabinetmaker Benjamin Randolph (1721–1791) of Philadelphia about 1765.

Pl. XXV. The Yellow Oval Room on the third floor, directly above the Blue Room (Pl. XXXVIII), was designed as a formal drawing room, the function it serves today. James Monroe once owned the painted and stenciled maple settee and matching armchairs, which were made in Philadelphia c. 1815. Flanking the door are a pair of late eighteenth-century gilded English looking glasses and a pair of gilded, marble-topped console tables made in France during the reign of Louis XVI.

Pl. XXVI. The carved and gilded armchairs beside the fireplace in the Yellow Oval Room are stamped by the Parisian furniture maker Jean-Baptiste Claude Sené (1748–1803). Above the early nineteenth-century Carrara marble mantel hangs *Sun in Summer*, painted by the American impressionist Daniel Garber (1880–1958). It is on loan from the Pennsylvania Academy of the Fine Arts. Pieces of presidential porcelain and early nineteenth-century European porcelain are displayed in the cupboard. The rug is a Turkish Hereke of the late nineteenth century; the chandelier is French, c. 1820.

Pl. XXVII.   This mahogany desk-and-bookcase stands in the private sitting room at the west end of the third story. Made in Maryland c. 1800, it is flanked by two (of a set of four) mahogany side chairs of about the same date which were probably made in Massachusetts.

Pl. XXVIII.   This room on the third floor was made into a private dining room for the president and his family in 1961. The mid-nineteenth-century French wallpaper is entitled *The War of Independence*. Fanciful scenes of the American Revolution were surprinted on a background printed from the same blocks as the wallpaper in the Diplomatic Reception Room (Pl. VIII). The American mahogany sideboard of c. 1820 is believed to have belonged to Daniel Webster. On it are two silver coffeepots made in Paris by Martin Guillaume Biennais (1764–1843), part of a service that Andrew Jackson bought in 1833 from the baron de Tuyll, then Russian minister to the United States. The dinner plates are from Lincoln's Royal Purple state service.

Pl. XXIX.   The gilded beechwood pier table now in the Entrance Hall was made in Paris by Pierre Antoine Bellangé (1758–1837). It is part of the set of furniture James Monroe ordered from France for the Blue Room in 1817. All the pieces but the pier table were sold at auction in 1860. (See also Pls. XXXVIII, XXXIX.) Monroe also ordered the gilt-bronze mantel clock on the table from Paris in 1817. The case, surmounted by a figure of Minerva, was made by Thomire et Cie; the dial is signed by Louis Moinet the Elder (1768–1853). The tall gilded English looking glass dates from the late eighteenth century. The bronze light standards were acquired during Theodore Roosevelt's renovation of the White House in 1902.

Pl. XXX. Chandelier, English, c. 1790. Cut glass and gilt bronze; height 72, diameter 46 inches. This superb chandelier illuminates the Entrance Hall (Pl. XXIX). Like many fine English chandeliers, it was found in India.

Pl. XXXI. The Green Room has been decorated in shades of green since the Monroe administration. It has had Federal furnishings since the Calvin Coolidge years (1923–1929), but most of the furniture now in place was acquired when the room was extensively refurbished in 1971 as a gift of the Richard King Mellon Foundation. At that time the Federal-style plaster-work, draperies, and window cornices were installed and the silk hung on the walls during the Kennedy administration was duplicated. The Carrara marble mantel is one of a pair ordered by President Monroe in 1817. The other one is now in the Red Room (see Pl. XXXVII). The gilded New York girandole of c. 1820 is decorated with a large American eagle and a very small British lion. The mantel is flanked by two mahogany worktables of c. 1810 attributed to Duncan Phyfe's shop (see Pl. XXXII); the rare mahogany pole screen at the right is attributed to the same shop, 1810–1815. An inscription on the frame of the easy chair indicates that it was made for Stephen Van Rensselaer of Albany by Phyfe's shop and upholstered in October 1811 by Lawrence Ackerman, one of Phyfe's upholsterers. Ackerman's name also appears in the inscription *Degez and Ackerman* on the frames of the window benches, which are thought to have been made by Phyfe c. 1810. The mahogany-veneer and satinwood deck-and-bookcase of c. 1815 is one of the few case pieces attributed to Phyfe's shop. An ingenious mechanism draws the cylinder front into the case as the writing board is pulled out, as it is in this view. Above the desk-and-bookcase hangs *Mosquito Net*, by John Singer Sargent. The table partly visible in the right foreground is described in the caption to Plate XXXIII. On it are a Sheffield-plate coffee urn of c. 1785 once owned by John and Abigail Adams and a pair of silver candlesticks made by Roch-Louis Dany of Paris in 1789. In 1803 James Madison, then secretary of state, bought the candlesticks from James Monroe.

Pl. XXXII. Worktable attributed to Phyfe's shop, New York City, c. 1810. Mahogany; height 28¼, width 23, depth 16 inches. Such ingenious worktables incorporate many drawers and storage compartments. This example and a similar worktable attributed to Phyfe's shop (on loan to the White House) flank the fireplace in the Green Room (see Pl. XXXI).

Pl. XXXIII. The ormolu chandelier in the Green Room was made in France c. 1810. The sofa, flanking drop-leaf tables, and sofa table are all mahogany, and all are attributed to the workshop of Duncan Phyfe, 1810–1820. On the wall above the sofa are a life portrait of Benjamin Franklin painted in London in 1767 by the Scottish painter David Martin (1737–1798) and Ferdinand Reichardt's *Philadelphia in 1858.* Over the door is a portrait of James Madison (1751–1836) painted from life in 1816 by John Vanderlyn (1755–1852) for James Monroe. On the right-hand wall is Gilbert Stuart's portrait of John Quincy Adams (1767–1848) executed in 1818, when Adams was secretary of state. It was the gift of Adams' namesake in 1970, as was the companion portrait of Mrs. Adams. Below the portrait of Adams is *Rainbow in the Berkshire Hills,* by George Inness (1825–1894). The marble-topped pedestal table is one of a pair attributed to Phyfe, c. 1815.

Pl. XXXIV. The Red Room was furnished as a drawing room in the Empire style during the Kennedy administration. The American mahogany-veneered sofa at the right was made 1815–1825. The unusual *guéridon* in front of it is shown in Pl. XXXV. Above the sofa hangs *View of Rocky Mountains*, signed and dated 1871 by Albert Bierstadt, which is on loan to the White House from the Barra Foundation. To its left is one of a pair of eighteenth-century gilded wooden sconces made in England for the American market. The life portrait of Dolley Madison (1768–1849) on the adjacent wall was painted by Gilbert Stuart in 1804 and is believed to have hung in this room in 1813. It is on loan from the Pennsylvania Academy of the Fine Arts. Below it is *Still Life with Fruit* of c. 1850, one of two paintings by Severin Roesen (w. in America 1848–c. 1872) in the room (see also Pl. XXXVII). Beneath the paintings is one of a pair of rosewood card tables in the room possibly made by Thomas Seymour (w. alone 1804–1843) of Boston, c. 1815. The portrait of John F. Kennedy (1917–1963) visible through the doorway was painted by Aaron Shikler (b. 1922) in 1970. Under it is a French Empire sofa purchased in 1803 by James Monroe and probably used by him in the White House. It is on loan from the Philadelphia Museum of Art. The rug is a wool and cotton reproduction of an early nineteenth-century French Savonnerie carpet.

Pl. XXXV. *Guéridon* labeled under the top by Lannuier, New York City, 1815. Mahogany with satinwood inlay, bronze and brass mounts, and inlaid marble top; height 29¾, diameter (of top) 26 inches. This extraordinary example of Lannuier's work is used in the Red Room (see Pl. XXXIV).

Pl. XXXVI. The draperies in the Red Room were designed by Edward V. Jones, architectural consultant to the Committee for the Preservation of the White House, and are based on early nineteenth-century designs. The marble bust of Martin Van Buren (1782–1862) was modeled by Hiram Powers (1805–1873) in Italy in 1840, and is one of three busts the artist made of Van Buren, who sat for him in 1836. The mahogany secretary of c. 1815 beneath the bust is the only one attributed to Lannuier. It is on loan from Mrs. James G. Balling. The mahogany sofa table is also attributed to Lannuier, c. 1810. To the right of the table is an early nineteenth-century French armchair that is believed to have been used in the White House before 1900 and subsequently sold.

Pl. XXXVII. The Carrara marble mantel in the Red Room matches that in the Green Room (see Pl. XXXI). The late eighteenth-century brass andirons in the Red Room are American. On the mantel shelf is a gilt-bronze clock made in Paris by Pierre Joseph Gouthière (1732-1812 or 1814). Above it hangs Henry Inman's portrait of Angelica Van Buren. To the right of the mantel is a mahogany music stand of c. 1830, appropriately enough in a room which was frequently used as a music room in the nineteenth century. In front of the music stand is a mahogany sofa with gilded dolphin feet, c. 1825, which represents the high point of American Empire furniture making. Over the door hangs a portrait of Alexander Hamilton (1757-1804), the first secretary of the treasury, painted c. 1805 by John Trumbull (1756-1843). It is one of eight replicas that Trumbull made of the head in the full-length portrait of Hamilton he executed for New York's City Hall in 1805 (illustrated in ANTIQUES for November 1976, p. 1031). To the right is a portrait of Martin Van Buren painted by Francis Alexander (1800-1880), 1830-1840. Below it is Severin Roesen's *Nature's Bounty*. The card table matches the one shown in Pl. XXXIV.

Pl. XXXIX. Armchair made by Bellangé, Paris, c. 1817. Gilded beechwood; height 38½, width 25½, depth 20½ inches. The chair is part of the set of furniture Monroe ordered from France for the Blue Room in 1817 (see Pl. XXXVIII). Monroe specified mahogany furniture, but his agents in Paris felt that gilded furniture would be more appropriate for the White House. All the pieces in the set except the pier table shown in Pl. XXIX were sold at auction in 1860. The seven chairs from the set now in the Blue Room and one sofa have been acquired since 1961.

Pl. XXXVIII. The oval Blue Room has almost always served as the principal formal drawing room in the White House. It is directly above the oval Diplomatic Reception Room (Pl. VIII) and below the Oval Yellow Room (Pls. XXV, XXVI). The Blue Room was decorated in the French Empire style under James Monroe and contains some of the furnishings he ordered from France in 1817: seven chairs made by Pierre Antoine Bellangé (see Pl. XXXIX) and, on the mantel, a bronze clock made by Denière et Matelin. The room has been known as the Blue Room since Martin Van Buren had the furniture covered in blue satin damask. The room was refurbished in the French Empire style in 1972 through the generosity of Mrs. James Stewart Hooker. The consulting architect of the restoration was Edward V. Jones, who redesigned and renewed the ornamental plasterwork and designed the elaborate draperies in the room based on nineteenth-century French pattern books. The wallpaper was reproduced from a fragment of a French paper of 1800. On the left is a copy by Adrian Lamb (b. 1901) of a portrait of James Monroe painted by Gilbert Stuart, 1818–1820, which is in the Metropolitan Museum of Art. Beneath the portrait is one of a pair of English neoclassical side tables, 1785–1790, on loan from the Corcoran Gallery of Art. The Carrara marble mantel, 1810–1815, is more elaborate than the similar mantels in the Green Room and the Red Room. It was installed in 1972 to replace the oversize mantel placed in the Blue Room under Theodore Roosevelt. Above the mantel hangs a gilded looking glass made in New York c. 1815, flanked by one of two pairs of French gilt-bronze sconces of c. 1810 in the room. To the right of the door is the only known portrait of Mrs. James Monroe (nee Elizabeth Kortright; 1768–1830), painted by an unidentified artist in London in 1796. The large oval rug was woven in Peking c. 1850 for a French palace.

Pl. XL.   The East Room, designed by Hoban to serve as "the Public Audience," or reception, room, has always been used for large gatherings of all sorts. Union troops were quartered in the room during the Civil War, and the bodies of Abraham Lincoln and seven other presidents have lain in state here. The room was not completed until 1829 and was renovated in the present neoclassical style by McKim, Mead and White in 1902. The Steinway piano was presented to Franklin D. Roosevelt in 1938. The portrait of John Quincy Adams in the corner was painted by George P. A. Healy (1813–1894) in 1857 and is one of seven portraits of presidents painted by Healy now in the White House. The likeness of Martha Washington (1731–1802) by Eliphalet F. Andrews (1835–1915) is a composite of life portraits. It was painted in 1878 as a companion to Gilbert Stuart's portrait of George Washington, which also hangs in the room.

Pl. XLI. The architectural ornaments in the State Dining Room were installed by McKim, Mead and White during Theodore Roosevelt's renovation of the White House in 1902. The marble mantel is decorated with American bison heads. It is a reproduction of the one installed in the room in 1902 which is now in the Truman Library in Independence, Missouri. Above the mantel is Healy's 1869 portrait of Abraham Lincoln. The pair of vases on the mantel was purchased by Monroe in 1817, as were the gilt-bronze fruit basket and mirrored, gilt-bronze plateau, which measures thirteen feet, six inches when fully extended. The plateau and fruit basket are attributed to Denière et Mateiin of Paris. The gilt-bronze candelabrum (one of a pair) had been added to the White House collection by the end of the nineteenth century.

Pl. XLII. The Family Dining Room is located next to the State Dining Room. The mahogany sideboard was made in New England, 1800–1815; the mahogany linen press, in Annapolis, Maryland, c. 1790. The latter once belonged to the family of William Paca, a Maryland signer of the Declaration of Independence. The silver plateau on the table was made in New York City c. 1804 by John W. Forbes (c. 1781–c. 1838), who also made the two other known American examples of this form. The silver tureen on it is one of two made by Jacques Henri Fauconnier (1776–1839) of Paris that were purchased by Monroe in 1817. The portrait of Theodore Roosevelt's second wife, Edith Carow Roosevelt (1861–1948), was painted by Theobald Chartran (1849–1907) in 1902.

Pl. XLIII. Desk-and-bookcase, Baltimore, 1800–1810. Mahogany. Height 9 feet, 2½ inches; width 89½; depth 22¾ inches. This imposing cabinet stands in the main corridor on the ground floor. Inside the top section are examples of the porcelain used by various presidents and their families, as well as a silver cake basket made by Robert Garrard (1758–1818) of London in 1803, and two silver cruet stands made by Roch-Louis Dany of Paris. The silver once belonged to the Madisons.

Pls. XLIV, XLV. North façade (top) and southeast corner (bottom) of the White House.

Selected Bibliography

Andrews, Alfred. "Some Nineteenth-Century Windows." *The Magazine Antiques* (August, 1946): 90-93.

Brightman, Anna. "Window Curtains in Colonial Boston and Salem." *The Magazine Antiques* (August, 1964): 184-87.

Butler, Joseph T. "Two Documented Nineteenth-Century Rooms." *The Magazine Antiques* (June, 1958): 551-53.

Comstock, Helen. "Paintings as Documents." *The Magazine Antiques* (November, 1950): 366-68.

Cooper, Wendy. "The Purchase of Furniture and Furnishings by John Brown, Providence Merchant, Part I: 1760-1788." *The Magazine Antiques* (February, 1973), 328-39.

_____. "The Purchase of Furniture and Furnishings by John Brown, Providence Merchant, Part II: 1788-1803." *The Magazine Antiques* (April, 1973): 734-43.

Cummings, Abbott Lowell. *Bed Hangings, A Treatise on Fabrics and Styles in the Curtaining of Beds, 1650-1850.* Boston: The Society for the Preservation of New England Antiquities, 1961.

_____. *Rural Household Inventories Establishing the Names, Uses, and Furnishings of Rooms in the Colonial New England Home.* Boston: The Society for the Preservation of New England Antiquities, 1964.

Fowler, John and John Cornforth. *English Decoration in the Eighteenth Century.* Princeton, N.J.: The Pyne Press, 1974.

Garrett, Elisabeth D. "Parlors A-Plenty: Pictorial Documentation of American Parlors, 1792-1845." Houston, Texas: Theta Charity Antiques Show Catalogue, 1979.

Little, Nina Fletcher. "An Approach to Furnishing." *The Magazine Antiques* (July, 1956): 44-46.

_____. *Country Arts in Early American Homes.* New York: E. P. Dutton, 1975.

_____. *Floor Coverings in New England Before 1850.* Sturbridge, Mass.: Old Sturbridge Village, 1967.

_____. "Joseph Shoemaker Russell and His Watercolor Views." *The Magazine Antiques* (January, 1951): 52-53.

Lynes, Russell. *The Domesticated Americans.* New York: Harper & Row, 1957.

Montgomery, Florence M. "Room Furnishings as Seen in British Prints from the Lewis Walpole Library, Part I: Bed Hangings." *The Magazine Antiques* (December, 1973): 1068-75.

_____. "Room Furnishings as Seen in British Prints from The Lewis Walpole Library, Part II: Window Curtains, Upholstery, and Slipcovers." *The Magazine Antiques* (March, 1974): 522-31.

Myers, Minor and Edgar Mayhew. *American Interiors.* New York: Charles Scribner's Sons, 1980.

"New Yorkers at Home." *The Magazine Antiques* (January, 1966): 106-11.

Nylander, Jane C. *Fabrics for Historic Buildings.* Washington, D.C.: Preservation Press, 1977.

Peterson, Harold. *American Interiors.* New York: Charles Scribner's Sons, 1971.

Praz, Mario. *An Illustrated History of Furnishing.* Translated by William Weaver. New York: George Braziller, 1964.

Roth, Rodris. *Floor Coverings in Eighteenth-Century America.* Washington, D.C.: Smithsonian Institution Press, 1967.

Rumford, Beatrix. "How Pictures Were Used in New England Houses, 1825-1850." *The Magazine Antiques* (November, 1974): 827-35.

Schiffer, Margaret B. *Chester County, Pennsylvania, Inventories, 1684-1850.* Exton, Penn.: Schiffer Publishing Co., 1974.

Seale, William. *Recreating the Historic House Interior.* Nashville, Tenn.: American Association for State and Local History: 1979.

Sprackling, Helen. *Customs on the Table Top.* Sturbridge, Mass.: Old Sturbridge Village, n.d.

Thornton, Peter K. "Room Arrangements in the Mid-Eighteenth Century." *The Magazine Antiques* (April, 1971): 556-61.

_____. *Seventeenth-Century Interior Decoration in England, France and Holland.* New Haven: Yale University Press, 1978.

Index